On Being a Christian
A Personal Confession

by

Henry Hamann

NORTHWESTERN PUBLISHING HOUSE
Milwaukee, Wisconsin

Second printing, 1998

Library of Congress Card 95-71847
Northwestern Publishing House
1250 N. 113th St., Milwaukee, WI 53226-3284
© 1996 by Northwestern Publishing House.
Published 1996
Printed in the United States of America
ISBN 0-8100-0578-6

CONTENTS

Church's Commission 116; The Teaching of
the Two Kingdoms 118

PREFACE

Henry Hamann was a member of the Lutheran Church in Australia. After serving a short time in the parish ministry, he entered the teaching ministry. He served in various capacities at Concordia College and Seminary in Adelaide and at Luther Seminary, North Adelaide, South Australia. Hamann had close connections with the Concordia seminaries in St. Louis and Fort Wayne where he received several post-graduate degrees and served as guest lecturer. He is the author of several commentaries and books on various topics.

Henry Hamann, a staunch Christian and confessor of the faith throughout his life and ministry, had plans for writing various manuscripts in his years of retirement. Several commentaries were in various stages of preparation, but the first work finished was this manuscript setting out his personal statement of faith.

That faith, however, faced a stern, unexpected test in the last few months of 1988. Soon after finalizing this manuscript in July 1988, he went to the United States for what was to be a year of guest lecturing. A few short weeks later, he was informed that a terminal illness had begun to ravage his body. After continuing with his lecturing assignments until late November, he was able to return to Australia by Christmas but died a few days later on December 30, 1988.

INTRODUCTION

Readers will, no doubt, appreciate knowing from the outset what prompted this book, and what they are likely to find in it. This volume tries to present the Christian faith from the viewpoint of one who, as a convinced Lutheran, holds that to be a Lutheran and to be Christian are not in any way matters in tension. They are the words of one who is a Lutheran because he is a Christian—of one who, if he were not a Lutheran, would not be a believer of any kind—of one who sees the only logical alternative to his commitment to the Christian Lutheran faith to be Epicureanism in its popular form: "Let us eat and drink and be merry, for tomorrow we are dead."

Perhaps I should expand a little on these rather clipped statements.

Christian First

I do not mean to say that it is more important to be a Lutheran than to be a Christian. If a Christian is properly described as one who is united with Christ by true faith in him, then no church affiliation of any kind can be placed on a level with it, let alone on a level above it. To be a Christian, in the sense of accepting the Christian faith, is to be in the only condition in which salvation is possible.

Unfortunately, *Christian* is by no means always used in the sense in which I have just used it, and it is because of implications found in other uses of the term that I make the statement that I am a Lutheran because I am a Christian. Two such implications I want to mention briefly and critically. One often hears the idea, variously expressed, that *it is more important to be a Christian than to be a Lutheran.* This statement is used in two ways, which I would like to mention briefly and critically.

I am sure that many who express this thought do so to excuse their complete non-commitment to the Christian faith. I have vivid recollections of one such person whom I came to know early in my ministry. Religious instruction in state schools was just being introduced in South Australia, and all parents were asked to indicate on the information form what church they belonged to, and what denominational class they expected their children to attend. One prominent man in the community said that he did not belong to any denomination, and that he did not want any religious instruction for his children. Yet he wanted himself to be listed as a Christian! Christian in such a context is so loose in meaning as to lose all meaning; almost every person and every opinion could be described as Christian. In such a context, the sentence "It is more important to be a Christian than to be a Lutheran" becomes meaningless twaddle.

There is another possible meaning which that quoted sentence could have. It could be a very boastful claim, a sign of an inner spiritual arrogance.

"You're only a Lutheran—I am a Christian, occupying a spiritual state far in advance of yours." In that case, the claim would remind us of those people in Corinth who, by claiming to be Christ's, wished to show their superiority over the members of other factions who called themselves by Paul or Peter or Apollos (see 1 Corinthians 1:11-13).

Those Christians who have their own personal commitment to the Christian faith will not misunderstand me when I say, "I am a Lutheran because I am a Christian." They will know that my strong commitment to the Christian faith leads me to the Lutheran confession of it because I see in such confession the true and appropriate expression of that faith.

The sentence "I am a Lutheran because I am a Christian" asserts (1) that the Christian faith is clearly revealed, (2) that it can be grasped and understood, (3) that it can be accurately stated, taught, and confessed, and (4) that this has been done in traditional Lutheranism. It is a further consequence of this conviction to hold that convinced members of other denominations would think exactly the same way about their view of the Christian message—and, thinking that way, would reject my views which are specifically Lutheran. It is only for such persons—those who take seriously their own view of Christianity and that of Christians who disagree with them—that I have any real respect. The big enemy of the true Christian faith is compromise, toleration, the spirit that we *all* are right—as if the important thing is not to be Lutheran but to be Christian without any denominational confession whatever.

Christian and Lutheran

I would now like to return to the personal statement with which my very first paragraph concluded, for it calls for some clarification. I said that I am a convinced Lutheran, one who holds that to be a Lutheran and to be a Christian are not in any way in tension.

The word *Lutheran* is often misunderstood, however. Lutheran there, and throughout this book, refers to a person or group that strictly holds to the Confessions of the Lutheran church when both their positive and negative statements are taken seriously. There are many Lutherans and Lutheran churches in the world to whom that definition no longer applies, and of this sad fact the reader must be aware. I also often speak of "the Lutheran," and this has a meaning in accordance with the definition just given. It means a person who knows accurately and accepts what the Lutheran Confessions teach, and who knows and accepts the kind of life that is harmonious with and consistent with that teaching. In a way, "the Lutheran" refers to the ideal Lutheran. Sometimes, a more general, popular use of the word *Lutheran* may be necessary. When I use phrases such as "some Lutherans maintain" or "there are Lutherans who," I imply a decline from the true historical Lutheran position.

No Acceptable Alternative

In my first paragraph I also voiced my view that Epicureanism is the only logical alternative to my Christian Lutheran faith. You may well wonder why. Well, this is the sort of abrupt comment I often make; it's the way I see and say things. But, at the same time, it is no idle comment; it is seriously meant. It is related to two contrasts: The one is the contrast between the Lutheran church and other churches, and the other is that between the Christian faith and all other religions.

The first contrast implies that if I believe, as I do, that the gospel or the Word of God is witnessed to purely and truly in the Lutheran Confessions, then there is no point in thinking of forsaking the Lutheran church to seek membership somewhere else. On the one hand, what is true and good in other churches can always be acknowledged as such and made use of (like the excellent Anglican prayers and other liturgical material). On the other hand, what makes any of the other churches distinctively what they are (such as papal authority in the Church of Rome) simply has to be rejected by the Lutheran —and membership in that church must likewise be rejected. For me as a convinced Lutheran, there is no acceptable alternative to Lutheranism in the various other denominations; therefore, the only logical alternative seems to be abandonment of the faith in favor of Epicureanism.

The second contrast implies that there can be no rival of any kind to the Christian faith. God became a human being in Jesus Christ once and for all. *"Salvation is found in no one else, for there is no other name under heaven given to men by which we must be saved"* (Acts 4:12). Christianity is simply in a class by itself among the "religions." It claims to be God's revelation to us, and that claim is acknowledged as true by the Christian. But this, in effect, puts all other religions into another class altogether: *human* endeavors to get to God or to worship him. And all such human attempts are worthless; God dwells in a light that no human person can approach. So, such religions may vary as to their human excellence, but none of them can be regarded as a true way to get to God or to worship God. For this latter purpose, they are all to be rejected completely.

So if there is, in fact, no way from us to God, and if the Christian claim to be a revelation from God is rejected, what is left? Only the enjoyment of this life for the brief time we are here before we die—in other words, Epicureanism. The same conclusion is reached when a life after death is denied, no matter by what religious group or individual.

Popular and Personal

This book, as a whole, is not meant to be scholarly in the sense of being for theologians only, and so is not a book teeming with theological words and speculations. It is hoped that no scholarly position has been neglected; however (and this must be stated right here) the writer's view of the Bible—that it is God's errorless revelation—would eliminate even that claim to scholarliness in the minds of most of my peers.

It is the interested Christian for whom this book is intended. It is for the person, lay or professional, who would like to have a commentary on the Lutheran faith in a continuous, concise, non-technical form. The book could well be likened to a lengthy sermon. And, like a sermon, it aims to persuade, convince, and win over the reader to the point of view of the writer.

What has been stated already has a further implication: The book has a personal quality about it. It is not a complete dogmatic or a textbook on the Lutheran faith; it is a presentation of the Lutheran faith from a very personal point of view. This is how I myself put the Christian faith in a summary, connected form. It is my answer to the question: "How would you, Henry, explain the Christian faith to the one who is interested in what makes you 'tick'?"

A careful reader will probably pick up another signal from these pages. There is in them an undercurrent of disappointment concerning the present state of Lutheranism in the world. As the late Dr. Sasse said very often, the ecumenical movement has destroyed dogma throughout the church. World Lutheranism is in a state of disintegration, and enthusiasm for the old faith seems to be disappearing, even in those parts of Lutheranism that used to make a great deal of their loyalty to the Confessions. Much is still said in those quarters about confessional Lutheranism, but a great deal of that talk is mere talk, pious conventionalism.

In the course of various drafts of this book, and as a result of lectures given here and there on its basic content, the hope has arisen that something of the old Lutheran conviction and faith may reappear. So I not only hope to give a clear account of my faith as a Lutheran; I pray that the Spirit of God may use what has been written to attract those who read it to a fuller faith—if not to faith itself—in the God who loved the world and gave his Son for its redemption and salvation.

CHAPTER ONE

WHAT IS
TO BECOME OF ME?

Every human being is confronted at some time or other with the riddle of existence: Who am I? What am I doing here in this world? What meaning is there to my existence? Am I only one among millions of people inhabiting this earth, and is this earth, in turn, a mere speck in an enormous, seemingly limitless universe? Where do I come from? And where am I going? And what will happen to me when I die?

There is no riddle of existence for those who hold that death is the end of everything. There is no riddle left—only meaninglessness. Riddles are meant to be solved; there is a solution to them even if some people never find that solution. But there can be no solution for the person who believes that everyone completely ceases to exist at death. Every person has, in that case, lived for nothing. The wise one and the fool, the supreme artist and the clod, the creator of beauty and the vandal—these are all on the same level with nothing to separate them. Of course, some people live on in an impersonal way through the influence their achievements have on future generations. But these persons too, according to the view being considered, come to the same final end— as the whole of the human race and the whole of history must also finally do. So according to this view, the whole of existence, as we human beings know it, starts with nothing and ends with nothing. That is not a riddle; that is madness.

Human Views and Solutions

Most people, so I believe, cannot really face the thought that their lives will have such a dismal end. The history of the human race supports this belief. In one form or another, all religions and philosophies have some teaching about the "last things," about the final destiny of the human race, of society, and of the world as a whole—just as they have a teaching about the first things, the origin of this universe and what it contains.

Such views or teachings of the end naturally differ very widely. The basic idea of immortality is widespread: the belief in personal survival after death. The ancient Egyptians are a good example of the conviction concerning such personal survival. The practice of mummification of the dead and of the provision of food for them point unmistakably to such a conviction.

Another commonly held view is that of reincarnation: The soul, which is immortal, inhabits a succession, a whole series, of bodies. This thought is prominent in the widespread religions of the East, Brahmanism and Buddhism. But it is also found among other peoples as well. It is found in the late Jewish teaching of the cabala. In pre-Christian

Europe it was advocated by the Greek philosopher Pythagoras and also by Plato, whose presentation of the idea may be read very pleasantly in his dialogue called *Phaedo.*

Modern interest in life after death is documented by such things as the phenomenon of spiritualism (the name of Sir Arthur Conan Doyle, creator of Sherlock Holmes, comes to mind) and the popularity of the book by Elizabeth Kübler-Ross, *On Death and Dying.*

Future Life Is an Axiom

It is simply a fact that human beings generally just cannot imagine that death is the end of everything, that their whole life with all its experiences, memories, achievements (which are sometimes very considerable) should simply be snuffed out with not a trace left. The human race has truly been described as the "eternal protestant" against death; we desperately refuse to accept what seems to be death's inexorable finality. That is why death is very generally regarded as not absolute or final, but as the transition from one particular world or kind of existence to another.

There are other arguments, besides that personal one, for the common conviction of a life after this life. The injustices of this life seem to call for a situation in which appropriate justice sets things right again. The American poet Longfellow reminds us that "though the mills of God grind slowly, yet they grind exceeding small." Unfortunately, in this life it seems to us that the grinding process is never complete. Too many injustices—very great and grievous ones, at that—have remained without appropriate judgment. The Old Testament psalmist complains about the prosperity of the wicked in contrast with his own experience which, in spite of his righteousness, was just the opposite:

> *This is what the wicked are like—*
> *always carefree, they increase in wealth.*
> *Surely in vain have I kept my heart pure;*
> *in vain have I washed my hands in innocence.*
> *All day long I have been plagued;*
> *I have been punished every morning*
> (Psalm 73:12-14).

After further consideration, the psalmist corrects this preliminary judgment, for he takes into account the end of the wicked and recalls the certain fact that God will take the believer into glory (see Psalm 73:17-24). But the adjusting of rights and wrongs, it is clear, remains a task for the future; it is not one that is brought about in the life we know.

All this hope for a future life and the conviction that it will come—a conviction based on various lines of argument—may, indeed, be dismissed as mere wishful thinking. But it is so universal, so persistent over the generations, that it takes on the nature of an axiom—something that is true whether we can prove it or not, something we accept as fact in order to live and exist at all.

Another Axiom: The Existence of God

Now, for me, it is beyond debate that belief in a future life confronts us with another axiom. The conviction concerning a future life, whatever its nature, demands the existence of a Person who is knowledgeable enough, mighty and powerful enough to establish the conditions of such a future life, a Person who is able to bring about a situation that will redress the injustices of this life. Conviction concerning a future life and conviction concerning the existence of God go together and complement each other. By bringing so close together the convictions concerning a future life and the existence of God, we are, in a way, using the desperate human need for an existence after this one as a support for the belief in the existence of God.

Something more must be said about the problem of the existence of God, partly because of the importance of the answer, and partly because it is related very closely to the subject of the second chapter: "How God thinks of me." There are really two questions concerning God which are involved at this point. The one is: Is there a God? And the second: Does he want me and, if so, on what terms?

The First Question: Is There a God?

About 20 or so years ago, the opinion was freely expressed that the first of the two questions was the really important one, upon which the second depended. For example, you may run across the following statements: "People of today no longer ask, 'How can I find a gracious God?' Their question is much more radical, more elementary; they ask about God as such, 'Is there a God?'" But is the radical question really about whether God exists or not? It will be granted at once that this is a natural question and, in its own way, it is an important question. On the surface, it seems to precede logically the question concerning God's relation to the world and to people.

However, even when this is granted, the question concerning God's existence is **not** the radical question. From the point of view of the Bible and also that of people in general, it is an unnecessary question—for every human being in his heart of hearts knows the answer: There **is** a God; God exists. It is only the fool who says in his heart that there is no God. One does not waste time debating what is an intrinsic part of human existence.

If, however, the question of the existence of God is taken up for serious investigation, we may find ourselves no closer to a final answer at the end of the big debate than at the beginning of it. The end of the very involved and complex philosophical argument concerning the existence of God can only be: The existence of God is very, very probable but, finally, it is not demonstrable.

Granting this outcome of the argument, one immediate consequence is that the question, Is there a God? becomes a most convenient red herring by which to escape the challenge of either the threats or the promises of the Word of God. For example, as soon as the question of my sin and my failure becomes too burdensome a thing for me, I can pose the question, But is there a God at all? and demand that that question be answered first—before I can be expected to take up seriously the questions of sin, guilt, a bad conscience, and divine judgment.

The Second Question: The Vital One

Even if it could be proved logically and philosophically—proved to the hilt—that God exists, we have gained nothing. We still know nothing about God's relationship to the world, to people: whether he is indifferent, jealous, hostile, loving, or what. All we have is knowledge which is, strictly speaking, futile and unusable. There is nothing radical or elementary about the question, Is there a God? It is a question which can be studied, discussed, debated with the greatest of personal detachment. One could treat it as one might treat a difficult chess problem; you might get excited about the question on an intellectual level but, finally, nothing depends on it.

The question concerning God's existence is the very opposite of an existential question, that is, a question in which the whole person and one's whole life and being are engaged and are at stake. On the other hand, the truly elementary and radical question is, How is God disposed toward *me*? Does he *want* me and on what terms? The marvelous Christian answer to that question is that **God justifies me**. And that is the subject of the next chapter.

CHAPTER TWO

HOW GOD THINKS OF ME

God's attitude toward the whole human race can be very fittingly described by the term *grace*; God is gracious to his whole human creation. In the Old Testament, we quite frequently find the phrase: to find grace (or favor) in the eyes of so-and-so. The person in whose eyes someone finds grace is always a superior: the king, a prince, God. So from the point of view of such a superior, grace implies loving and favorable condescension. *Favor, consideration, affection*: these three words together give a picture of the mind and heart of God toward all human beings. Frequent synonyms for *grace*—more or less equivalent —are words like *love, mercy, kindness.*

God Is for Us

This attitude of God is in no way static or passive in nature. God's attitude of love, mercy, and grace leads him to action, leads him to seek the real good, welfare, and happiness of human beings. So the Christian is one who holds that God is for him/her in every way, in every circumstance, now and in the hereafter. God is no enemy, no tyrant, no unfeeling or hateful God, playing around with human beings, treating them with indifference or contempt, like boys cruelly playing with flies (Shakespeare in *King Lear*). God is not like what the Greeks imagined their gods to be: careless of what happens on earth. A striking picture of that sort of god comes from the pen of Fitzgerald.

> We are no other than a moving row
> Of Magic Shadow-shapes that come and go
> Round with the Sun-illumined Lantern held
> In Midnight by the Master of the Show;
> But helpless Pieces of the Game he plays
> Upon this Chequer-board of Nights and Days;
> Hither and thither moves, and checks, and slays,
> And one by one back in the Closet lays.[1]

It is the Christian conviction that God is *for us* in every way—*in every way*. But it is necessary for me to concentrate for the present on the core aspect of God's being for us: that *God justifies me.*

It is often argued by pastors of the church that lay Christians have great difficulty in understanding the idea just referred to, that words like *justify* and *justification* are too hard for the ordinary person to understand. Now it is probably true that the words themselves do cause trouble, and that a sentence like "God justifies me" is an unusual one, a sentence often met by blank faces. But I do not believe that the idea itself is unusual or hard to explain. Public figures are continually defending themselves, their words, their actions, when others stand up in condemnation; and the common word for this defense is *justify*. So also, people are continually seeking justice in law courts, pointing out that their actions were right and proper, and that they should be acquitted of all charges against them and be declared "not guilty." This is just what justification describes—the one new idea being that God does the acquitting, the justifying. So the difficulty often seen in this terminology seems to me to be greatly exaggerated.

God's Justifying Act

The gracious, loving, merciful God justifies me—or has justified me. He treats me and regards me as one who is just and righteous, and as really being the kind of person God expects me to be. Later I am going to refer to both the problem and the mystery that are implied here.

At this point, it is important to realize that justification refers to the position or the status that people have in God's sight, in his judgment. It does not refer to their nature or to the kind of character that they have or are (whether, for instance, they are of good or bad character). To be justified by God simply means to be *regarded by him* as righteous, as just, as being in the right relation with him. We are faced here with a *fact*, a result of the judgment of God concerning human beings. In line with Scripture, the Lutheran church insists: God has justified me; I have his approval; I am in the right with him.

The Bible uses other terms to refer to the same basic situation between the Christian and God, and they can help to make us think as we ought in this matter of status, position, relationship. The Christian is described as being *a child of God* and, as such a child, also *an heir.* Children enjoy a legal position in the family, no matter what their character or conduct. The relationship of father/mother to child is a fixed one, and although parents on rare occasions renounce a child or children, the relationship is a permanent one. Being a child or heir of God has this same relational character about it. Of course, Christians should be accurately described as *adopted* children—they are not physical or biological children of God. But such adoption makes the objective, relational, legal character of their position even more obvious. Personal character is not the point; it is the decision, choice, objective verdict of God the Father that determines the relationship between the Christian and God.

Forgiveness, Reconciliation

Two other synonyms of justification must be mentioned, both because they are important in themselves and because they point directly to the problem and mystery implied in justification. These synonyms are *forgiveness of sins* and *reconciliation.* Saint Paul uses the thought of forgiveness contained in Psalm 32:1,2 as a direct proof or support for his statement in Romans 4:5 that God justifies the ungodly. Similarly, statements about reconciliation are directly parallel to statements on justification, as in Romans 5:9,10 and in 2 Corinthians 5:18-21. The thought of forgiveness of sins implies, of course, that human sin is a disqualification for acceptance by God. That of reconciliation goes even further in that it asserts a state of irreconciliation or enmity between the sinful human race and God. Both ideas point directly to the mystery in this whole matter: How can God justify human beings, make them his children and heirs, forgive their sins, become reconciled to such rebels?

The Reality of Sin

We have to look at this dark side of the whole matter more closely. The very strong terms in which sin is described in the Bible are often attacked by non-Christians. So also are the corresponding tones of repentant humility in which Christians see themselves before God. For example, such folk will condemn a text such as Matthew 7:11, *"If you, then, though you are evil, know how to give good gifts to your children,"* as a very great exaggeration. They also pick on such phrases as "I, a poor, miserable sinner" from the Confession of Sins in the Lutheran Common Service as a shameful and unnecessary low view of self. However, although the idea of the blackness and horror of sin is attacked in principle, it is actually granted by the very same people in practice.

Poets and philosophers often become very eloquent in their description of the nobility of human beings, of the spirit they can show, of the quality approaching the divine displayed in their greatest works of art and music and building and medicine and literature—and all-conquering science. The Greek poet Sophocles says at the beginning of one of his choruses in the *Antigone*: "Wonders there are many, but not one of them is as wonderful as the human being."

But people generally know very well that this divine creature is also very much of a devil. When the Bible says

> *There is no one righteous, not even one;*
> *there is no one who understands, no one who seeks God.*
> *All have turned away, they have together become worthless;*
> *there is no one who does good, not even one*
> (Romans 3:10,11),

well, everyone agrees. What person of history with a fair name (including Jesus) has not been debunked by biographers? You could not declare in company that either Mr. X or Miss Y was really a good person without being immediately contradicted by somebody. The point is, we know ourselves so well that we cannot permit anyone to get away with a good reputation. We just don't believe that a good person exists; there are bound to be feet of clay around. Imperfection and sin—and even serious vice—are there waiting to be revealed and brought to general knowledge. Revelation of evil in supposedly good people has happened so often that we are confirmed in our opinion of the wickedness of humankind.

It is often stated by theologians that the thought of human corruption is something accepted only by Christian people, that the greatness of evil and wickedness in the human race can be grasped and accepted only through the action of the converting Spirit of God. But I know from personal encounter that there are downright enemies of the Christian faith who have no trouble at all with the thought of a general human wickedness. They know the world; they know history; they know the human race and all the evil it has wrought in the past and the atrocities it continues to perpetrate in the present; and they have no doubt at all that the human race is at heart bad, corrupt, rotten, and that all human supposed virtues are really only vices in disguise. There are plenty of people around who believe all this of specific nations or races of people on every continent of our globe. Psychoanalysis is a good example of how the human person is often seen in this world: a seething mass of instinctive, selfish passions kept in control with great difficulty. Even what looks like a virtue is only an unacceptable desire in an acceptable form.

Rebellion against God

The truly terrible nature of sin, however, becomes evident only when it is seen as rebellion against the good God. Here too what is often claimed is contrary to what is actually the case. The human race is said to have a desire for God, a desire to be in union and fellowship with him. The words of the church father Augustine are often quoted: "Thou hast made us for thyself, and our heart is restless until it finds its rest in thee." At the profoundest level, these words are undoubtedly true. But on the level on which they are frequently quoted, they are true only when the god which people have in mind is a human fabrication, a false god.

When you present the true God to them, the God revealed in Christ, the God lying as a babe in the manger, the God dying in shame and pain on the cross, and also the God who reacts with wrath and punishment and damnation against the sinner, then the resulting reaction is far, far different. Then what we get is the comment of the French philosopher Voltaire that such an infamy should be rooted out from the human race. Or we get the poetic words of Edward Fitzgerald:

> Ah, Love! couldst thou and I with Fate conspire
> To grasp this sorry Scheme of Things entire,
> Would not we shatter it to bits—and then
> Re-mould it nearer to the Heart's Desire!

And again, but more violently this time:

Oh, Thou, who didst with Pitfall and Gin
Beset the Road I was to wander in,
Thou wilt not with Predestination round
Enmesh me, and impute my Fall to Sin?
Oh, Thou, who Man of baser Earth didst make,
And who with Eden didst devise the snake;
For all the Sin wherewith the Face of Man
Is blacken'd, Man's Forgiveness give—and take!

God Justifies Sinners

The human being as biblically described: this evil, wicked, sinful monster whose total potential for self-excellence is turned to base, ignoble ends; this rebel against God, this enemy of the good Creator—this is the one whom God justifies, whom God by a solemn judicial verdict declares to be right before him. It is this sinful being whose sins are taken away; it is this rebel who is called to be child and heir; it is this enemy whom God seeks and reconciles to himself. In all cases, it is human beings *as they are*.

That is why Saint Paul says that God justifies "the ungodly," **not** the good and noble and righteous and godly. And this same thought Jesus uttered well before Paul: *"I have not come to call the righteous, but sinners [to repentance]"* (Matthew 9:13). This justification of the ungodly surely turns all normal standards of right and wrong, of justice and injustice, of law and order, upside down. It is more than a mystery or paradox; it seems almost midsummer madness. But, so says the gospel, and so says the Lutheran: This is the only way you can be saved; if you don't want to be saved as a sinner by a freeing, judicial verdict of God, you cannot be saved at all, and you will perish in your sins.

However, it must now be shown how God can act in this unheard-of fashion. How can God remain holy and just in himself and, at the same time, grant free and full forgiveness to the rebellious sinner? To answer that, we must now speak about Jesus Christ.

CHAPTER THREE

GOD FOR ME
IN JESUS CHRIST

From the very beginning of Christianity, Christians have held that Jesus Christ is both God and man in one person.

In the Apostles' Creed, the church confesses Jesus Christ to be

> [God's] only Son, our Lord, who was conceived by the Holy Spirit, born of the virgin Mary, suffered under Pontius Pilate, was crucified, died, and was buried. He descended into hell. The third day he rose again from the dead. He ascended into heaven and is seated at the right hand of God the Father almighty. From there he will come to judge the living and the dead.

The so-called Nicene Creed of A.D. 381 expands somewhat on the divine nature of Jesus Christ and declares concerning him that he is

> . . . the only Son of God, eternally begotten of the Father, God from God, Light from Light, true God from true God, begotten, not made, of one being with the Father. Through him all things were made.

Lutherans have made these ancient confessional statements part of their own Lutheran Confessions, repeating the statements in the old creeds in approximately the same form in the *Augsburg Confession* and in the *Smalcald Articles,* and expanding on the personal union between the divine and the human at length in the *Formula of Concord* in two articles: Article VII (The Holy Supper) and Article VIII (The Person of Christ).

The Mystery: God with Us

The Incarnation, that is, that God became flesh (a human being) in Jesus of Nazareth, is a completely unfathomable mystery. As such, it has naturally been repeatedly attacked and rejected down the centuries by people within the church, as well as by people outside of it. However, denial of the Incarnation puts a person outside the Christian church.

I have no intention of debating the matter here. But it is worth pointing out that to deny that the man Jesus of Nazareth was at the same time truly God in the one person does not eliminate the difficulty of understanding the person of Jesus. You may get rid of one difficulty only to come up against another.

Who Is Jesus Christ?

If Jesus of Nazareth was (is) not true God, what are we to make of his many sentences that imply he was divine or that directly make that assertion? Sentences like the following come to mind:

> *All things have been committed to me by my Father. No one knows the Son except the Father, and no one knows the Father except the Son and those to whom the*

Son chooses to reveal him. Come to me, all you who are weary and burdened, and I will give you rest (Matthew 11:27,28).

I am the light of the world (John 8:12; see also 9:5).

The reason my Father loves me is that I lay down my life—only to take it up again. No one takes it from me. . . . I have authority to lay it down and authority to take it up again (John 10:17,18).

I and the Father are one (John 10:30).

Most striking of all the examples, probably, is Jesus' reply to a demand of his disciple Philip:

Philip said, "Lord, show us the Father and that will be enough for us." Jesus answered: "Don't you know me, Philip, even after I have been among you such a long time? Anyone who has seen me has seen the Father. . . . Believe me when I say that I am in the Father and the Father is in me" (John 14:8-11).

What sort of person can this Jesus be that he speaks in this way? If he was not God, he was quite, quite mad. But then his many sentences, like those in the Sermon on the Mount, and also many others besides, do not give the impression of madness at all, but of quite exceptional wisdom. Was Jesus, then, a devil of the deepest dye, a matchless hypocrite, one who clothed the most shameful lie—*"I and the Father are one"*—in a cloak of profound spiritual wisdom?

One could, of course, get rid of all this difficulty by taking a completely negative, critical line.

One could deny that Jesus ever said anything approaching the sentences that have been cited, deny that he ever made any claim which suggested that he was more than an ordinary human being. One could insist that after his death his followers invented all these claims and assertions about him. One could do this by rewriting all the records concerning him, chiefly the four gospels, on the basis of a strong personal and biased point of view, without any shred of support in the written materials of the infant church. One must be aware in doing this, however, that one is engaged in an activity that can only be called illegitimate elimination of historical evidence.

Others less critical might say, "Granted that Jesus Christ was born, say, in 4 B.C. and died in A.D. 30 and now has risen to be with his Father, as God and man eternally, and is who the Christian creeds assert. What are we to say about his life, death, and resurrection? What was the work that he accomplished?"

With some simplification, it may be said that there are three main ways in which the life of Jesus has been assessed.

Some Say: Jesus Is Only a Great Example

There is, first of all, the view that Jesus Christ is the great example for mankind, the great example of what a human life should be like and how all human beings should live. Jesus is described as the man who lived unreservedly for others and set all selfishness aside. Reference is made to the actual words of his teaching that proclaim this thought, as in the Sermon on the Mount in Saint Matthew's gospel, chapters 5–7. Writers point to his deep and sincere concern for others as shown by his practical help and acts of healing, or his evident sympathy and understanding for the despised and rejected, such as tax collectors, prostitutes, and other outcasts of society.

In contrast with this soft and gentle side of the man, equal praise is directed to his stern morality, his incorruptible devotion to what is right and true, his hatred of all sham, humbug, hypocrisy, and self-righteousness. No less to be commended is his conduct and his confession of the truth which led him to his trial, condemnation, and death as a criminal on a Roman cross. One could say that Jesus was the ideal, righteous man suggested and described by the Greek philosopher Plato (428/7–348/7 B.C.) in his *Republic*, the just man whose righteousness is the pure and sincere doing of what is right for its own sake, apart from all self-seeking.

> And at the side of the perfectly unjust man let us place the just man in nobleness and simplicity, wishing, as Aeschylus says, to be and not to seem good. There must be no seeming, for if he seem to be just he will be honored and reward-ed, and then we shall not know whether he is

just for the sake of justice or for the sake of honors and rewards; therefore let him be clothed in justice only, and have no other covering; and he must be imagined in a state of life the opposite to the former. Let him be the best of men, and let him be thought the worst; then he will have to be put to the proof; and we shall see whether he will be affected by the fear of infamy and its consequences. And let him continue thus to the hour of his death; being just and seeming to be unjust.[2]

"Here, in Jesus, is your ideal man, in reality and not merely in imaginative construction," say those who see in him a pattern and a model. "Now you go and live the same way!" So Jesus becomes a person to be imitated in our lives. And if we all did this, who could doubt that the world would be a far better place in which to live?

Quite frequently, what is pointed out as unique about Jesus is that he was so intimately attached to God—what we might call his "God-consciousness." Many people claim that Jesus' use of the term *Abba* particularly points to this intimacy. Here was a man—so the thought runs—whose closeness to God was such that he dared to speak to him in the completely trusting way in which children call their father "Daddy"! Such a picture of Jesus is really a variation of the theme that Jesus is the great example and model for human beings.

Others Say: Christ Merely Reveals God

A second view of Jesus is that he lived to show people the true nature of God. Many (if not most) people picture God as an angry being who is to be feared and dreaded, the picture of an enemy or tyrant. This attitude is one of the effects of a bad conscience or of the fear and awe that must accompany the thought of the great difference between the frail human being, who lives for a day and then perishes, and the holy, eternal, mighty God. Or it can be brought about by a combination of both.

Such a picture of the angry God is claimed to be what Jesus Christ was sent or chosen by God to do away with. It is claimed that a false idea and picture of God has to be removed, that the human race has to be enlightened as to what God is really like. He is not a wrathful and hateful God at all, but a God of love and kindness, concerned only about our welfare and happiness.

Jesus Christ, so this view suggests, showed the true nature of God in his words and deeds. Accordingly, he associated with tax collectors and sinners; he forgave the sinful women who came to him (Luke 7:36-50 and John 8:1-11) and did not condemn them. That is what God is like. In the parable of the prodigal son (Luke 15:11-32), they continue, we have the real relationship between God and human beings presented in a classical way. The younger son, after wasting all his inheritance in a self-indulgent, debauched way of life, becomes aware of the sorry state to which his style of life has brought him. He remembers his father and his home, where he couldn't possibly be worse off than he is now. He is full of remorse and shame at what he has done. But when his father sees him in the distance on his homeward way, he rushes to meet him, won't listen to any stammered words of regret, and treats him like an honored guest, and even better than that. There is nothing but love in the father's heart. The past is not only forgotten; it's just not there at all. That's what God is like, they say. So Jesus came to teach human beings what they did not know and could not know. Jesus is the human race's great Enlightener as to the true nature of God and as to the state of God's attitude toward all people.

However, there are serious objections to both these views of Jesus' work and importance for the world. These objections may be summed up in the Latin phrase *nondum considerasti pondus peccati* (you have not taken into consideration how great is the weight of sin). Such consideration results in a somewhat different picture of Jesus than what has been set out above.

We Need More Than an Example, More Than a Revealer of God's Kindness

In the first case, the human race does not need another example of goodness, of virtue, of noble living; it has models of behavior in word and example enough and to burn. The big problem is not ignorance of what is right and wrong, of what we should do and not do, of how we should live and not live. The problem is the sinful nature of the human race, our inborn inability to do the right and to avoid the wrong. We approve the better, but follow the worse.

At best, there is the ability in human beings to conform to the standard of behavior that society as a whole regards as acceptable—when it suits us! Living the moral life is never better than outward conformity. If human beings are as described in the previous chapter, then even the most perfect example of moral behavior, as we have it in Jesus Christ, cannot change matters one whit. In fact, the perfect example can only be a condemnation: "This is how you ought to be (that is, like Jesus), but now look at yourself and see what you are." It is no wonder that Jesus, the perfect man, was crucified. He would be crucified or treated worse today too. Every generation, Jew and Gentile, would have done precisely the same as those who did bring about Jesus' death. The sinful human being just cannot abide a good person, let alone a perfect one.

On the other hand, what sort of picture of God emerges if Jesus' task is merely to show God as the God of love and grace and kindness? Is that the only attitude God has toward a very sinful race?

Does sin make no difference to him? Can he merely hide his face from it all? Can he ignore all the ghastly public crimes of our modern age? Does he ignore our private sins and cruelties that are beyond number and description—sins we deflect attention from by gloating over the greater sins others have committed? Can God simply hide his face and say, like an indulgent father: "Boys will be boys"?

Is God really like the father described in the poem by Coventry Patmore called *The Toys*? Don't let the beautiful poetry keep you from seeing the shallow sentimentality of what is said here. A father has punished his little son who disobeyed him seven times, striking him and sending him off to bed unkissed. Later he relents, goes to see his son, and is upset by the sight of various objects on the bed, used by his son as a means to comfort himself. The father prays, as his bedtime prayer, the following:

> So when that night I pray'd
> To God, I wept and said:
> Ah, when at last we lie with tranced breath,
> Not vexing Thee in death,
> And Thou rememberest of what toys
> We made our joys,
> How weakly understood
> Thy great commanded good,
> Then, fatherly not less
> Than I whom Thou hast moulded from clay,
> Thou'lt leave Thy wrath, and say,
> "I will be sorry for their childishness."

However powerfully Jesus is pictured as the great ideal and model and pattern of human living, or as the revealer of the true mind of God, these pictures just fail to convince. They are untrue to the great realities of God and of human sin. Neither of these supposed ways of saving human beings deal with sin effectively. These pictures of Jesus have been produced from within the human mind; they are pictures of what we ourselves would like to be the case. But, as all people are liars, so these views of what Jesus means for the human race are lies and deceptions also.

The views concerning Jesus that we have been considering—this should be clearly noted—are not completely wrong and without value. However, they become so if they are taken as the *complete* answer to the question: What did Jesus do?

The Bible Portrait of Jesus

The specific Christian answer to this question is that **Jesus changed the situation**, or relation, **between God and people**; he created a new state of affairs. Various comparisons are used in the Bible to describe the new situation that Jesus brought about.

To start with, Jesus is described as redeemer, and his work as **redemption**. In general terms, redemption amounts to liberation, to a setting free. Christ set all people free from what previously enslaved them or kept them captive. If we become specific, then the word *redemption* brings in the idea of paying a price. You redeem your property from a pawnbroker by paying the price that is put on your property. Prisoners of war in earlier days were redeemed, set free, by the paying of a certain amount of money. A kidnapped person could be described as redeemed by the payment of the ransom demanded. So the death of Jesus is the ransom price that redeemed sinful humankind from sin and its consequences.

Another frequently used picture for the work of Jesus Christ takes us into the realm of **sacrifice,** and to terms like *priest, blood,* and *Lamb of God.* Guilty people are released from the guilt, pollution, and punishment of sin by a sacrifice offered in their stead. Jesus Christ, in his death, was that sacrifice.

Again, the idea of **reconciliation** is used for the work of Christ in the Bible and in the proclamation of the church. Between God and his human creation there exists enmity, hatred: Human beings hate God, and God is full of anger against human sin. Some people don't like thinking or speaking about the anger of God; such talk is said to be sub-Christian. However, one can't get rid of the idea as easily as that, and it is an idea that runs right through the Scriptures. What is needed in such a situation of hatred and anger is reconciliation, removal

of the conflict that separates. This God did. He reconciled the rebellious world to himself. (It is never,
by the way, declared in the Bible that God "is reconciled" to mankind; *he* did the reconciling, and he did
it by sending his Son, Jesus Christ.)

Death in Our Place

In all these pictures of what Christ has done
for people, or of what God has done for all people
through Christ (those phrases are interchangeable),
it is always the death of Christ that is the determining factor. His death is the ransom price in redemption; his death, the sacrifice; his death, the means of
reconciliation. Because of that, his death is
described by the term *vicarious,* which means *in
place of others.* Christ died instead of and in the place
of sinners; what they deserved, he suffered; what
they owed, he paid. The statements of Saint Paul
are quite drastic in this regard. He can say that
"God made him who had no sin to be sin for us"
(2 Corinthians 5:21). So not only our death was put
on Christ, but also our guilt; our sin was accounted
to him, so that God treated him as sin personified.
Paul can also say, *"Christ redeemed us from the curse of
the law by becoming a curse for us"* (Galatians 3:13).
This took place at his crucifixion. Because Christ in
this way assumed our sin, guilt, curse, death, and
the full condemnation of the law of God, the new
relationship between God and us was brought

about. Sin has been adequately dealt with—yes, more than adequately. God's law of love and holiness has not been ignored; it has been conceded its full right. God remains righteous and just in himself, and at the same time he can pardon sinners, justify them.

His Life, His Death, and His Resurrection

It may be good at this point to make clear how I intend references to the death of Christ to be understood. There are two clarifications to be made here: one in respect to the life that preceded Jesus' death and the other pertaining to the resurrection that followed that death.

First, the repeated references to the death of Christ do not ever have the intention of suggesting that the life of Jesus Christ was really of no consequence. A number of important passages in the New Testament refer to the **obedience** of Jesus Christ, such as Philippians 2:8 and Hebrews 5:7-9. This emphasis on the obedience of Christ leads us to see that the whole of Jesus' life—culminating in his death—makes up his great work for us. The whole of Jesus' life plus his death is his obedience.

There are two sides of the coin here: Christ's actual doing the will of God throughout his life in obedience and Christ's acceptance of the punishment of the law in accordance with the Father's will (and his own too, so closely were his will and that of the Father united). Both in his actions and in his suffering, he was obedient to his Father.

In addition, we can say quite truthfully that Jesus' obedient death was the proof of his obedient life. So there is a point to using the term *Jesus' death* as a shortcut for the more complete and more comprehensive expression of obedience in life and death.

The reference to the death of Jesus Christ is a shortcut in another sense as well; it is short for his **death plus his resurrection**. Without the resurrection, the death of Christ would have been only a sad event, tragic for his friends, a release for himself, but not something of any special consequence for anybody else. As Paul puts it: *"If Christ has not been raised, your faith is futile; you are still in your sins"* (1 Corinthians 15:17). On the other hand, all talk of a resurrection is meaningless without a previous death. In a word, the references to Jesus' death in this writing are shorthand for the sentence of Saint Paul: *"Jesus our Lord . . . was delivered over to death for our sins and was raised to life for our justification"* (Romans 4:24,25).

Divine Love Abounds

It is only natural that there should be strong objections to this view of the work of Jesus Christ. The whole idea of the wrath of God, as pointed out before, is distasteful to some. God, they hold, should not be thought of as getting angry and flying into a

49

rage like human fathers and mothers and others in authority. The whole transaction, they continue, seems unspeakably grisly: the divine anger being appeased by a human death, by the shedding of the blood of a sacrifice. What is more, for all the talk of law and justice, what sort of justice is that which punishes the innocent for the guilty and lets the guilty get off scot-free? This whole transaction, they say, can only be a fairy tale, a legal fiction—but never, never reality.

Such objections are, in part, based on misconceptions. God's anger does not have to be pictured as a violent, uncontrolled, undignified human passion. Even human anger is not always of that kind. There is such a thing as righteous indignation, when anger is aroused by cruelty and injustice. The world is full of anger of this kind, although it must be admitted that it rarely exists in a pure state and is usually fused with a less noble emotion. The righteous anger of God is expressed in such things as the flood, the destruction of hardened Jerusalem, other catastrophes engulfing nations, and even eternal punishment. But, for all that, it is never to be separated from divine love. The great act of redemption was set in motion by divine love. Divine love overcame the demands of divine wrath in Jesus Christ. God took sides with us mortals against himself, as one scholar has put it. The wrath of God looks quite different when viewed in combination with God's love.

So also, the vicarious death of Jesus—the innocent Jesus dying in the place of guilty humanity —can be defended. The sacrifice of Christ for sinful humankind was a voluntary one. Naturally, it is unjust to punish an innocent party for those who are guilty if that punishment is compulsory. But it is quite a different matter if there is a voluntary offer to undergo such punishment for others. The whole human race honors those who give their lives for, in place of, others. *"Greater love has no one than this, that he lay down his life for his friends"* is a sentence often quoted from Saint John's gospel (15:13). To it we can add another from Paul's letter to the Romans: *"But God demonstrates his own love for us in this: While we were still sinners, Christ died for us"* (5:8). Even on the basis of human judgment, it could not be shown that such voluntary assuming of another's guilt and punishment implied an act of injustice or that there was a legal fiction involved. And in the great transaction in which Jesus Christ is the central figure, God, not just a man, was acting for our benefit—and God lies beyond the sphere of human judgment.

The crucial point of this for the defense of Christian teaching of the redemption is that, unlike the first two views, this view actually does deal with realities: the reality of sin, the reality of the divine law, and the reality of the love of God. These realities are taken completely seriously in the Christian teaching of redemption. There is no sentimentalizing, no soft-pedaling, no glossing over of unpleasant matters. The law's demands are met, God's wrath is appeased and averted, and his love is given free course to pardon and forgive.

No Other Way

Nothing but a changed situation was necessary if there was to be salvation for the human race. No other view of the work of Christ except the one just outlined actually does supply such a changed situation. The relationship between God and his human creation is different now because of the life, death, and resurrection of Jesus Christ. Although foretold in prophecy, and so not absolutely new, this all-embracing, once-for-all event occurred with and in Jesus Christ.

The Christian's confidence that God is for us in every way—for us, first of all, as the God of forgiveness and justification—is solidly, immovably grounded in the redeeming work of Jesus Christ. Luther has given classic expression to this thought in his explanation of the Second Article of the Apostles' Creed:

> I believe that Jesus Christ, true God, eternally begotten of the Father, and also true man, born of the virgin Mary, is my Lord. He has redeemed me, a lost and condemned creature, purchased and won me from all sins, from death and from the power of the devil, not with gold

or silver, but with his holy, precious blood and with his innocent suffering and death. All this he did that I should be his own, and live under him in his kingdom . . . just as he has risen from death and lives and rules eternally. This is most certainly true.

CHAPTER FOUR

THROUGH CHRIST
I AM A FREE PERSON

Early in Chapter 2, the statement was made that God is for me **in every way**. This claim was not explained or developed or explored in detail at that place. Consideration of it was deferred in order to point out at some length the particular way in which God is for me, the believer; to point out how God is for me in forgiveness, justification, and adoption; to point out how God is for me in that way because of the substitutionary work of Jesus Christ, because of his life, suffering and death, and resurrection for me in my place. With that task done, it is now the time and place to show how this "for me" is all-embracing, how God is for me in every way.

There is a key text in Saint Paul for this assertion: *"What, then, shall we say in response to this? If God is for us, who can be against us? He who did not spare his own Son, but gave him up for us all—how will he not also, along with him, graciously give us all things?"* (Romans 8:31,32).

Once you have granted the initial premise or condition (if God is for us), the Christian logic of these verses cannot be faulted. It is unthinkable that the God who sacrificed his Son (or, to say the same thing, that the Son who sacrificed himself for the sinful and rebellious human race) should think of the human race in any other way but in keeping with his great sacrifice for it. God has given his Son into the depths of woe and degradation, into the death of crucifixion, into the depths of misery beyond imagination—for us.

Freed from all Evil

A gift like that is the guarantee that God's dominant impulse is his love and kindly concern for all who belong to the human race. He cannot mean me harm: so argues the one who believes that such a gift has been given in Jesus Christ. God is my friend, in no way my enemy. He is my friend in everything that happens to me, both in what pleases me and in what people would generally grant to be good, and *also* in what seems to be the opposite—what causes me pain and distress, grief and sorrow. Since God can *only* want my good and my welfare, whatever happens to me is good, and is something to thank and praise God for. *"The LORD gave and the LORD has taken away, may the name of the LORD be praised"* (Job 1:21). And again: *"Shall we accept good from God, and not trouble?"* (Job 2:10).

Luther's *Small Catechism* works with this argument. While Luther does not there present the argument in actual words, the results of the argument are plainly stated. In his explanation of the Second Article (cited at the close of Chapter 3), Luther confesses our faith in Jesus Christ, Son of God and Son of man, the one who is humankind's redeemer through the giving up of his own life. Earlier, in his explanation of the First Article, Luther penned the following confession of God's gracious attitude and actions:

> I believe that God created me and all that exists, and that he gave me my body and soul, eyes, ears, and all my members, my mind and all my abilities.

> And I believe that God still preserves me by richly and daily providing clothing and shoes, food and drink, property and home, spouse and children, land, cattle, and all I own, and all I need to keep my body and life. God also preserves me by defending me against all danger, guarding and protecting me from all evil.

Although the First Article comes before the Second, the underlying theological argument runs in the other direction, from the Second Article to the First, from the supreme demonstration of the love of God in Christ Jesus to the love that accompanies the whole of the Christian's life.

That Luther actually thought in this way can be seen everywhere in his works, but nowhere more winsomely and attractively than in his writing *The Freedom of the Christian.* This little writing was produced in 1520, in the midst of Luther's most tumultuous years, and dedicated to the ruling pope of that time, Pope Leo X. The theme of the writing is that the Christian by faith is lord of all things, subject to nobody and nothing, but that at the same time the Christian is subject to everybody by love. What is being developed in this chapter of mine obviously owes a great deal to Luther's ideas in that charming little book.

Now, if it is right and true that God is for me in every way, and if I, the Christian, know it to be valid in faith, then I am certainly a free person. Even the unbeliever will grant the truth of this argument for the Christian. Everything that happens is controlled by God's loving concern for me. Everything works for my good. I am, as Luther says, lord of all things. There are certain consequences for day-to-day living that are the immediate result of this conviction.

Freed from Worry and Care

The first consequence is a cheerful and optimistic attitude toward life: I need not worry about myself, my life, my health, my business, my family. In any case, I obviously can't live forever, nor would anyone in his right mind want to, for in that case, the greater part of life would mean interminable years "without teeth, without eyes, without taste, without everything." The most any sensible person would want would be to get along happily and well for the normal span of life.

The faith that God is for me in every way clearly makes brooding, care, worry, and anxiety sub-Christian; such things are incompatible with, and stand in contradiction to, that faith. It would be fine if all soul-destroying care were no longer an issue in the Christian life, but the ideal is not the reality, as Luther has emphasized elsewhere by reminding Christians that they are at the same time sinner and saint. But the point I wish to make is that the faith that God is for me in every way is God's antidote to the worry that undermines inner joy.

Normal reactions to good and bad experiences, to pleasant and unpleasant happenings, to what normally gives happiness and what does not, still remain, but they need not take over and dominate the personality. Where the faith that God is for me in all things is dominant in life, there is quiet confidence, an underlying joy, an overarching optimism. The life experiences of Christians do not differ fundamentally from those of non-Christians; what is true of the latter is, or can be, true of the former. And life experiences—good and bad—may vary in a very great measure from person to person. But *the attitude* to all such experiences, *that* can be very different. And that difference is due to the aforementioned faith that one person has and lives by and another does not have. As a Christian, I can accept with serenity and patience everything that happens to me when *"I live by faith in the Son of God, who loved me and gave himself for me"* (Galatians 2:20).

Freed to Have Worth and Dignity

Since God is for me in all things, I also suddenly find myself invested with worth and dignity. There is no doubt that many people go through life with a low assessment of themselves. They feel unimportant and inferior; they almost despise and hate themselves; they compare themselves with others to their own disadvantage: Others are smarter, more energetic, more popular, better looking, healthier, more successful in life. Other people, in some cases, seem to have almost all the advantages: They have everything and can do everything, while the rest, by comparison, have very little going for them and are "losers" through and through. None of that sense of inferiority need overwhelm the Christian, the one who is in Christ Jesus.

If God is for me in every way, if he in his love regards me as his child and heir, then plainly I have worth and dignity. I can hold my head up and look every man and woman in the face. I don't have to lord it over anyone; but neither do I have to go around like some slave avoiding everyone's eye and acting as if I have to apologize to everyone for living. I may not be very important in the world's eyes, and I shall certainly be forgotten as soon as I am dead, but I am still a person. I am I, and my God in Christ has called me to be his child—and that dignity no person can take from me.

Freed to Love Others

Since God is for me in all things, I have the ability to be there for my neighbor. I am given the power to love, to be unselfish, to be a true, moral person. At an earlier stage in this book, it was pointed out that the whole human race lies under the power and control of sin and wickedness; how our knowledge of sin in people generally, and in ourselves in particular, makes us doubt whether anyone is really good and makes us agree with God's judgment, despite our own innate rebellion against him: *"There is no one who does good, not even one"* (Romans 3:12). But now, it is necessary to insist that the one in Christ is a person who really has been given the ability to be unselfish, and so, to serve with genuine sincerity, without any hidden motives for doing so.

How can this be, or why should it be so? The answer is simple enough. The reason behind the inability to love and the movement toward sin is an ingrained selfishness in all human beings. Each of us, by nature, is the center of his own universe. Everything has importance for me only in so far as it concerns me. Even if millions lose their fortunes and their lives, what of it if mine is still intact? People today, at least in the western world, have even made a virtue and a praiseworthy principle of this selfishness: Every man and woman is to do his/her "own thing," and no one else is to dispute that right. Of course, when two wills clash, and two little, wholly independent realms come into conflict, then there is the devil to pay!

But now through Christ, by the conviction that God is for me in all things, the power of selfishness is broken, for **I can't have any more by selfishness than I have by faith**. Everything is taken care of by God: all my needs, all my security, all my difficulties. Nothing is outside the range of God's gracious will for me and for my life. So I am really set free from all my worries and concerns for my own skin. I am free and ready to serve my neighbor. I can live for others with complete sincerity.

No other like motive for a life of love and service can be found anywhere else, not in any other religion, not in any philosophy. Laws of good conduct—and on this level the Ten Commandments are included too—can only feed selfishness. There is no more selfish person than the moral individual intent on personally securing an eternal, happy future by doing what the law of God demands. The fulfilling of the law, the more seriously and conscientiously it is carried out, becomes more and more an exercise in selfishness. But for those who are in Christ, all that is cared for and attended to already. They are forgiven persons; they are justified for Christ's sake, and there's no worry on that score. And as God is *for them* in every way, so they, as free children of God, can be *for their neighbor—for others—* in every way. It is only when the faith that God is well disposed toward them grows weak and feeble and departs or is forgotten that they revert to the selfishness that is theirs by inheritance and membership in a sinful race.

The great example of this love bubbling forth out of complete devotion to God is, of course, Jesus Christ. We have already pointed out that the redemption and salvation he won for us does not consist in the example set for human beings to follow. But the example, it must be repeated, is there as well. No freer person can be imagined than Jesus of Nazareth; no person could be more truly described as "the man for others." It was pointed out earlier that in Plato's *Republic* we have a picture of the ideal person whose righteousness is pure giving of himself for others. The picture painted there—even up to the kind of end that such a person could expect—is quite an amazing anticipation of what Jesus of Nazareth really was. But the picture from Plato's imagination is still a long way from the perfection that was Jesus. The example of Jesus—the free man who loves and the loving man who is free—is there for every Christian to follow.

Freed in Our View of Work

What freedom to love means can be seen particularly well in one special aspect of Christian living: the work they do, their job, occupation, calling. To start with, Christians view their calling, their job, their occupation, as the chief way in which they can serve, help, and benefit their fellowmen. After all, our occupations take up a very great portion of our lives. Next to sleeping, we spend most of our time each day working. If we want to serve our fellowmen—really serve them—then clearly we must view our work as the way in which we can do this most effectively and completely. This understanding leads Christians to work at that for which they are most suited; they realize that they can serve their neighbor far better as a good carpenter or mechanic or plumber, or as a good wife and mother, than as a poor teacher, an indifferent physician, an incompetent minister. By contrast, non-Christians never give this matter even a passing thought; their whole attitude toward work is prompted by self-interest. They turn to that job that gives the best income, or the most security, or desirable honor and prestige: "No dead-end job for me; I must keep up with the Joneses!"

The right attitude toward employment: that it is the opportunity for concentrated and continuous service to their neighbor, marks Christians also as they do their work. They strive to be conscientious about their work, reliable in carrying out their tasks, and so on, for with that attitude toward their work, they know they are serving their neighbor as best they can. The ramifications of all this are endless. But they cannot be pursued further here.

One thing, however, does need a comment: Given the conditions of modern employment in big businesses and large factories, it is probably very difficult for Christians to act as they know they should and as they want. Specious rules drawn up by bosses and labor unions tell them how much (or, usually, how little) they ought to do and how fast (or, usually, how slowly) they ought to work. Bucking the rules and the establishment can very easily lead them into great difficulties. Antagonism from other workers, loss of employment, or even attacks on their person persuade them to think again about their Christian convictions and to adopt the low ideals of the marketplace and the business world.

How to act in such situations has to be determined from case to case, and no all-embracing rules can be given. However, Christians cannot sacrifice their ideals and neglect the love they owe their fellows. They must witness to these ideals, even if the hard facts of necessity force them to act in a way that falls short of what freedom to love calls for. Freedom and the love that freedom inspires do not in this life reap the rewards that they deserve. But since the love of God remains the great constant, Christians will go on believing and will go on loving, no matter what.

Freed to Enjoy God's Gifts

Since God is for me in all things, I have also the freedom to make use of and to enjoy all that this world offers. After all, the same God who has loved me in Christ is the one who created this world and all that is in it. The enemy of God and of people creates nothing; he merely tries to ruin and destroy the good that is already there. So Christians in freedom will not permit their freedom to use the world to be challenged. They will not permit others to make the world less roomy and commodious than it in fact is. A narrowing and cramping of the world is just what is brought about by the many prohibitions: "You must not eat this or that or something else! Nor must you drink this beverage or that! You must not engage in this or that work or activity!" The prohibitions are endless, and they come from pietism, both religious and secular. The free Christian is superior to these endeavors to make the world smaller and narrower than it is.

Only one consideration will lead the Christian to forgo this aspect of his freedom. That is the demand of love for others, which must come first at all times. As a Lutheran Christian, I won't allow my freedom to become a danger or a nuisance or a distasteful thing for my neighbor. After all, freedom means the right or permission to use or not to use what this world offers. Permission or right to use this or that is no command or compulsion to do so. So the decision freely made to use or not to use what is there is, in each case, the exercise of the freedom the Christian has. Tricky situations can arise, as, for example, when other people (even fellow Christians) insist unreasonably that I give up *my* freedom so that they can have *their own way* on some matter. This little book is not designed to answer in detail how I should act in such cases. And the answer may differ from case to case. However, if the basic freedom is under attack, then my action must be one that preserves the right and not that which betrays my freedom.

Since God is for me in all things, I am free also as I face the future and the question of what is to happen to me at the end of this life. But that will require a special chapter by itself. For the moment, it is necessary to look more closely at what has been claimed in this chapter about the effects of faith in the life of the Christian.

Freedom Flowing from Faith

I have insisted on the freedom of the Christian. I have made much of the liberation of the Christian from the bondage of a bad conscience and the guilty feelings aroused by sin. I have claimed that Christians prove triumphant over all the many problems and cares and miseries of this life, and that, in spite of the worst that can happen to them, they can still be happy at heart because of the God who has demonstrated his love for them in Jesus Christ. I have also claimed that the Christian faith—and only that faith—makes it possible for Christians to really love and serve their neighbor in unselfishness. I have asserted, further, that faith in Christ and in the love God has for me gives me a sense of personal worth and dignity. That same faith gives the Christian the freedom to use all that this world has to offer—yet with a sense of responsibility to God and others.

It is important to note that in making these assertions, I have been speaking of what is ideally the case, or of what should be the case for persons who are completely convinced that God is for them in every way, or of what is true of all Christians when their faith is dominant and in control.

If this is not kept in mind, then it is possible for two things to happen. Skeptics, after reading what has been asserted here, can point at all the professing Christians they know, for whom very little of what has been written here seems to be true or to be in evidence. They can go on to argue, therefore, that what I have claimed is an empty claim devoid of truth, since the facts of everyday life and experience involving Christians are directly opposed to this claim. The second possible result is that even many Christians can be undeservedly afflicted with a bad conscience as they observe in themselves very little of the life that I have said faith makes possible. They see in themselves far too little of unselfish love for their neighbor. Or they are full of worry and anxiety as they look at their lot in life and as they think of the future. Or they feel little of the personal dignity that Christians are said to have. They observe, finally, far more hesitation than freedom in enjoying the things God has put into his creation for us.

The solution to the problem lurking here has already been hinted at. There is no doubt that the faith that God is for me in all things leads directly to the results mentioned in this chapter. Where that faith is active and prominent, these results do take place. The Christian in faith will live in the way described. But the rub, of course, is that Christians are not controlled by faith every minute of their lives; Christians still remain the sinful beings described in a previous chapter. The Bible describes this aspect of the Christian as the "flesh," and the life in faith is called "spirit." There is, in effect, a continual struggle between flesh and spirit in the Christian. This explains a contradiction that is obvious to Christians themselves and observable also by non-Christians: the contradiction between what faith in complete control *would produce* as the Christian life and what so often *is produced* by Christians who are flesh as well as spirit.

CHAPTER FIVE

HOW I FACE DEATH
AND WHAT LIES BEYOND

God is also for me at my end, and after that. We have seen how the grace and mercy of God in Christ makes me a free person, for that gift is all-embracing. It takes care of my sin and guilt and moral imperfection. It makes all that happens to me in this world something that works for my good. It fits me to love and serve my fellowmen with complete sincerity and generosity. It puts the world and what is in it at my disposal to be used in freedom and love. It gives me personal worth and dignity. That is a great deal in anyone's language. But it still is not the full story of what I have in Jesus Christ by God's grace, for **my total future is taken care of as well**.

There is something incomplete about the gift of God as it affects me here and now. Most people would hold that what is claimed in these pages is complete fantasy. They hold that view because, externally, nothing—not a thing—indicates that the Christian faith, as it has been developed here, is actually directed to what is really and finally true. The experiences of believer and unbeliever in this life are precisely the same. Some people have a good life externally: They have plenty to live on; they reach a ripe old age, and nothing much ruffles the placid course of their existence. With others, the situation is quite the reverse: Hard luck dogs their every step; they apparently experience nothing but sorrow and disappointment of all kinds; they seem to attract trouble and misfortune as a magnet attracts iron.

But these extremes, as well as all conceivable in-betweens, are not related at all to faith or the lack of it. Believers and unbelievers are found in all these classes. Nothing that happens to all these groups indicates which persons within them belong to the group of believers and which do not. We could very well apply the words of the Preacher in Ecclesiastes 2:13-16 to this whole state of affairs, but we must substitute *faith* and *unbelief* respectively for *wisdom* and *folly* in the original.

> *I saw that wisdom is better than folly, just as light is better than darkness. The wise man has eyes in his head, while the fool walks in the darkness; but I came to realize that the same fate overtakes them both. Then I thought in my heart, "The fate of the fool will overtake me also. What then do I gain by being wise?" I said in my heart, "This too is meaningless." For the wise man, like the fool, will not be long remembered; in days to come both will be forgotten. Like the fool, the wise man too must die!*

Both Present and Future

It is in keeping with these experiences that the New Testament describes the gift of God as both "present" and "future." It is also common to refer to this distinction in a short formula: It is the difference between the "already" and the "not yet." In fact almost all the words or phrases which refer to the gift of God in Christ are used in this double way.

So the kingdom of God is already here, as Jesus said in Mark 1:15: *"The time has come. The kingdom of God is near* [that is, it is here]. *Repent and believe the good news!"* or in Luke 11:20: *"But if I drive out demons by the finger of God, then the kingdom of God has come to you."* (That is, it is here because I am at work. See also Luke 17:20.) But on the other hand, we are taught in the Lord's Prayer to say: *"Your kingdom come,"* a petition that also contains a clear reference to the future of God's kingdom.

Likewise, we are justified here and now, as many passages declare; but Paul can also say that we await *"the righteousness for which we hope"* (Galatians 5:5). Again, already now there is redemption in Jesus Christ, as Paul says in Colossians 1:14: *"in whom we have redemption, the forgiveness of sins."* But it is also true, as we read in Romans, that *"we ourselves, who have the firstfruits of the Spirit, groan inwardly as we wait eagerly for our adoption as sons, the redemption of our bodies"* (Romans 8:23). The same passage also shows that "adoption as sons," which is a present possession according to Romans 8:14-17, is also something to be awaited, as Saint John also declares: *"Dear friends, now we are children of God, and what we will be has not yet been made known. But we know that*

71

when he appears, we shall be like him, for we shall see him as he is" (1 John 3:2).

But what will the "not yet" be like? Do we know anything about it? The answer is: A little; some of this little is very definite, but much of it is vague and hazy.

Death marks the end of the "already" with its ambiguities; we enter into the "not yet" by resurrection. Death for the Christian is only a transition, hard and fearful as it may be. After death is the resurrection into a new life, the life into which Christ our Savior and Lord has already entered. Because he lives, we shall live also. This is a definite.

The other big definite is the perfection of the "not yet." There will be perfect happiness and holiness in the presence of God, whose sight or presence no human being could endure in the circumstances of this life. The new life of heaven will be perfect, for it will mean constant, unchanging, complete, and permanent enjoyment of fellowship with God. There will be no lapse or falling away from it, no loss of the perfect possession, no end of the perfect life.

We Know in Part

What is vague about the new existence are the details and the concrete aspects of that existence. Scripture contains pictures enough of the "not yet" state. These pictures are all drawn from the circumstances of this life. Those occurrences and conditions and possessions that give us pleasure here in this life are transferred, with some exaggeration, to the time and the world that are coming. We have pictures of a beautiful, perfectly defended city, of marriage and the wedding day, of a banquet of food and drink, of a delightful world of nature. With these pictures are joined all the negatives—the absence of all those things that cause us pain and sorrow and misery here in this world: *"Never again will they hunger; never again will they thirst. The sun will not beat upon them, nor any scorching heat. For the Lamb at the center of the throne will be their shepherd"* (Revelation 7:16,17). As for the body, *"The Lord Jesus Christ . . . will transform our lowly bodies so that they will be like his glorious body"* (Philippians 3:20,21).

There is no valid basis for the idea that Christians should not add their own imaginings to these pictures. A friend of my father's imagined heaven as a place where he could spend endless pleasant hours with my father in discussion, smoking a contemplative pipe, and drinking a good beer. Why not? This is valid as long as we continually realize that these are only pictures and not realities and that the realities will be far grander and more glorious than we can dream.

Focused on Christ's Return

The whole future of the "not yet" is tied up with the return of Jesus Christ. The Christian creeds speak of one of the purposes of Christ's return: "He will come again to judge the living and the dead" (the Apostles' Creed); "He will come again in glory to judge the living and the dead" (the Nicene Creed); "At his coming all people will rise with their own bodies to answer for their personal deeds. Those who have done good will enter eternal life, but those who have done evil will go into eternal fire" (the Athanasian Creed). The determining question of Christ at the judgment will be: "Did you really believe in me, or not?" The judgment will reveal each person as he/she was. There will be no deception any longer—no self-deception and no deception of others. Realities will be the order of that day—not talk, not appearance.

But why must Christ return in order for this to happen? Is judgment not possible in other ways? Why this particular office for Christ? Well, mankind judged Christ in the days of his flesh. The world has seen only his shame, loss, death, destruction.

> *Your attitude should be the same as that of Christ Jesus: Who, being in very nature God, did not consider equality with God something to be grasped, but made himself nothing, taking the very nature of a servant, being made in human likeness. And being found in appearance as a man, he humbled himself and became obedient to death—even death on a cross!* (Philippians 2:5-8).

The picture the world has seen of Christ has to be paired with another, that of glory and triumph.

74

Therefore God exalted him to the highest place and gave him the name that is above every name, that at the name of Jesus every knee should bow, in heaven and on earth and under the earth, and every tongue confess that Jesus Christ is Lord, to the glory of God the Father (Philippians 2:9-11).

It is also certainly fitting to give another reason for this: The person through whom the whole salvation of God for our race has come and by whom it was achieved should also be the one to judge whether it has actually been accepted by people, or rejected by them.

Faith's and Hope's Full Focus

Another very important thought, besides that of the judgment, is tied to the return of Jesus Christ: The Christian needs the hope of the return of Jesus Christ and what belongs to it, with all its consequences, in order to continue to live by the faith that makes up the Christian's existence. Only a final judgment, an unmistakable act of God—in short, the return of Christ, through whom God has from the beginning dealt with humankind—can give the demonstration that is needed to remove the ambiguity from this present life, where what is good and right does not always triumph, and where evil is not always put down. Leave faith without the hope of such a clear act of judgment, and faith would collapse. Faith is certainty and unshakable confidence, indeed, but it can be that only if it is linked with the hope that God will infallibly prove the reality of those things in which faith now trusts.

We can have no certainty if we are uncertain about this whole situation and if we are bound to remain so forever; such a faith could only be a gamble, a venture. It is doubtful whether any of our churchly activities would have value any longer if the future hope were removed from our faith. If there is no resurrection and no life after this one and if all earthly things and things human are meaningless, then the whole of religion and the whole of philosophy becomes unnecessary, and occupying oneself with it becomes a prodigious waste of time. The only alternative is the philosophy of Epicures: "Let us eat and drink and be merry, for tomorrow we are dead." In Melbourne 25 years ago, I heard a woman declare that she could "do nothing with the Christian hope." I told her I could not be a Christian without it.

I do not think that anybody who knows the Christian faith would want to deny the importance of the Christian hope of eternal life. If we grant the necessity of a final demonstration of the truth of the Christian faith, then the return of Christ is a necessity also. That demonstration cannot be put off indefinitely. In fact, the sooner the return, the better. This thought will become clearer when we compare the situation at the time of the New Testament with the situation of the church today.

The Timing of Christ's Return

The New Testament is full of sentences suggesting, or even stating quite directly, that the Lord Jesus would return and bring about the consummation of all things within the lifetime of the first Christian generation. There are some very striking sentences in this regard. Some are from Jesus himself, like the following: *"When you are persecuted in one place, flee to another. I tell you the truth, you will not finish going through the cities of Israel before the Son of Man comes"* (Matthew 10:23; see also 16:28). Indeed, it is not too much to say that the whole of the teaching of Jesus is permeated by the thought of the completion and nearness of the kingdom of God.

A similar situation exists in the writings of the apostles. As for Saint Paul, we have the words: *"According to the Lord's own word, we tell you that we who are still alive, who are left till the coming of the Lord, will certainly not precede those who have fallen asleep"* (1 Thessalonians 4:15; see also Romans 13:11). For Saint Peter, there is the sentence: *"The end of all things is near"* (1 Peter 4:7). For James: *"The Lord's coming is near"* (James 5:8). And for Saint John: *"Dear children, this is the last hour"* (1 John 2:18). The second-last verse of the Bible contains the message: *"He who testifies to these things says, 'Yes, I am coming soon.' Amen. Come, Lord Jesus"* (Revelations 22:20). With this closing sentence we must compare the congregational shout in 1 Corinthians 16:22: *"Maranatha"* (Come, O Lord).

Alongside this kind of material that is pointing to a quick, almost immediate return of Jesus Christ, we find many sentences that suggest that there is time left in history for the work of the church and its mission of preaching the gospel throughout the world. Many of these also go back to Jesus himself.

That combination of ideas is strange enough. Even more strange is that in the years following Jesus' death, there is no indication that the church was particularly perturbed by this state of affairs. There is actually only one passage that shows that any curiosity existed as to the delay of Jesus' return. This passage is 2 Peter 3:3,4, where mockers of the Christian faith are described as making use of that delay to call the Christian faith into question. (Modern scholars often paint quite a different picture of the state of affairs in the early church in respect to this matter. However, a simple and direct reading of the New Testament material yields the result just sketched.)

To proceed, it is clear that the state of affairs seen in the New Testament could not long continue. The problem of the nonreturn of Jesus Christ was bound to become more and more serious as time went on, and Christians today cannot possibly avoid or ignore the matter. The books of the New Testament could well have been all written by A.D. 70, when only 40 years—no great span of time—had elapsed since the death of Jesus Christ. But for us, more than 19 centuries have passed since then, and the protracted nonreturn of Jesus must be seen as a serious temptation to doubt the Christian faith, as has been hinted at already.

How to Understand Christ's Words

To a considerable extent, the problem is solved if we keep this fact in mind: Jesus frequently spoke in riddles. We often have to use considerable imagination and look beyond or deeper than the actual words used. Nobody in his right mind, to give one example, would dream of taking literally the advice: *"If someone strikes you on the right cheek, turn to him the other also"* (Matthew 5:39). To follow that sentence literally would be the surest way to get another blow in the face, and to arouse that anger that Jesus really wants the insulted one to allay and put an end to. Non-retaliation is the point of the sentence. In the same way, what Jesus intended in those arresting sentences referred to earlier (Matthew 10:23 and 16:28), and others, was not to give information about the time of the return, but to mark the utter necessity of the end, the return, the judgment, and the consummation of the kingdom of God. It was to make the point that Christians want the end to take place as soon as possible because of its absolute necessity.

Some Christians sense a danger in this necessary emphasis on the importance of the future for the Christian faith. They think—and the thought is certainly a natural and almost inevitable one—that a deep concern for the future can only disqualify human beings from a full participation in the tasks and the problems of life in the present. They can point to the New Testament for confirmation of their fears. The letters to the Thessalonians were written partly from Paul's need to correct believers in Thessalonica who gave up working because of their conviction that the end of the world was already present. The result of such idleness, even though entered into for pious reasons, actually happened: They looked for food and other items of support from their fellow Christians, poked their noses into other people's affairs, became busybodies and a positive nuisance. Paul had to speak sharply to them, as you can see from 2 Thessalonians 3:6-12.

Healthy Hope a Stimulus

But what resulted then from a keen sense of the end of the world and an earnest looking forward to it, and what some people expect to happen today, does not have to happen. The true understanding of the Christian hope and its relation to faith does not at all move in such a direction. The Christian hope, we have shown, is a support for Christian faith; in fact, it is Christian faith turned toward the future.

God for me in every way in the future is part of his being for me in every way in the present. We have seen that such a conviction leads to freedom, and freedom makes possible true, sincere love for the neighbor. Faith is always active and energetic in love (Galatians 5:6). The expectation of the future, as support for and part of faith, plays its part in the grand effect we have seen faith to have. Far from being a sort of featherbed in which the Christian can lie down and take his ease, the Christian hope is a springboard to action, hurling the Christian into even greater concern for fellow Christians and for others. Hope for the future, for death and the beyond, fits the Christian even better for this life, for love for his neighbor, and for the task of taking the gospel to all people, so that they too may be brought to salvation.

CHAPTER SIX

GOD'S WORD
AND MY FAITH

The question that naturally suggests itself at this stage of my presentation of Lutheranism is: Where does the faith come from that God is for me in every way, bringing me into a life of freedom for others? How does it come about in me?

The Spirit's Gift: Faith

The Lutheran replies emphatically that such faith comes from God alone, from his Spirit; it is not in any way a product of the Christian's own mind, intellect, or will. "I believe that I cannot by my own thinking or choosing believe in Jesus Christ, my Lord, or come to him. But the Holy Spirit has called me by the gospel, enlightened me with his gifts, sanctified and kept me in the true faith" are words familiar to Lutherans from the *Small Catechism* of Martin Luther.

A further question at this point leads us to views of the Christian faith that are distinctively Lutheran in their total impact, even though Lutherans and other Christian churches enjoy common ground on certain individual aspects. That question is: How does the Spirit bring about this faith, this love, this hope? Lutheran teaching rejects all or any *direct* influence or action of the Spirit on the heart of the Christian. The Spirit is not to be found in inner experiences or outward happenings of any kind, as though these experiences or outward happenings could be sure signs—or, indeed, signs at all—of the Spirit's presence and activity. **The Lutheran sees the Spirit tied by his** (the Spirit's) **own will to the Word of God.** Where the Word of God is, there the Spirit is—and there is no Spirit when the Word of God is not present. It is not that the Spirit of God *could not* be present anywhere else, but rather that we human beings *have no right to expect* him anywhere else. So this chapter, concerned as it is with the coming into being of the Christian life of faith, hope, and love, is concerned with what Lutherans call "the means of grace," the "channels" which the Holy Spirit uses to bring us God's grace: the Word of God and the sacraments.

The Spirit's Means: The Gospel

All revelation from God to us is by means of his Word. It has been customary in certain parts of the church to speak also of God revealing himself by means of nature (the existence of the world) and history. All that can be known through these factors is that a God exists. They reveal *"God's invisible qualities—his eternal power and divine nature"* (Romans 1:20). This, of course, is not without importance for it leaves all those given to idolatry and all atheists with no excuse whatever. But it can be called revelation only in some diluted sense, for everything that really is of consequence, how God as a person is related to this world and to those who live in it–all of that remains unknown. Revelation of this kind never leads further than to God as the great question mark, the "hidden God" (the *Deus absconditus*, as theologians like to call him). But God nevertheless!

The revelation of God is the speaking of God. True revelation exists only when **God speaks**. In his speaking in human words, he reveals himself in judgment and grace. His words are also necessary if we are to know his great acts for the benefit of mankind.

This speaking took place in different ways. *"In the past God spoke to our forefathers through the prophets at many times and in various ways, but in these last days he has spoken to us by his Son"* (Hebrews 1:1,2). The prophets spoke the Word of God; the apostles spoke it; Jesus spoke it; in fact, he is the Word of God in person. And countless men and women have transmitted the Word in one form or another to other people down through the ages.

> One must always keep in mind that the Word–
> or *a* particular word–exists in various forms: in
> the heart of God, going out of his mouth, com-
> ing to the prophet, heard by him, proclaimed by
> him, written in Scripture, read, learned, remem-
> bered, translated, accompanying the dying
> soul–always the same powerful and living Word
> (Hermann Sasse).

God's Written Word

In all these forms of the Word, a special place belongs to the *written Word* of God or the Holy Bible. This is so because all other forms of the Word preceding the written form have perished and are not recoverable by us. The oral word of prophets, apostles, and of Jesus Christ himself (who never wrote a word as far as we know, apart from a few words in the dust on one occasion) was not fixed for all time by tape recorders or other devices. And Jesus himself is not available to us for consultation as he was to the disciples. However, we have those words and pronouncements of the prophets and apostles and of Jesus Christ, which God wanted preserved for all time, recorded in the Scriptures of the Old and New Testaments.

This form of the Word is permanent, approachable, readily available; and as the permanent form of the Word, it is the source and authoritative norm for all preaching and teaching in the church of God. It is the original form of the Word for us and for the whole New Testament church to the end of time. There is no getting behind it to something more original and more authoritative.

Revelation in Law and Gospel

God reveals himself to us in his Word in two very different ways. On the one hand, he is the God who confronts the human race with his **law**.

He commands the good and right and forbids the evil and wrong. He reacts with strictness and severity against all transgression and flouting of his law. *"The soul who sins is the one who will die"* (Ezekiel 18:4). The transgression of the law is sin, and sin separates the soul from God eternally. On the other hand, he is the God who proclaims his grace and forgiveness, life and salvation, in answer to human sin. The message of grace and all blessing we call the **gospel**.

The definition just given of law and gospel indicates clearly that they are completely different in their natures. Luther even spoke of them as more than contradictory. They are both completely the Word of God, the revelation of the one God, but they perform two very different functions in bringing people to salvation.

The law performs a preparatory task (sometimes called God's "alien" or "improper" task). The service the law renders the gospel is to prepare the hearts of sinners to hear with joy the promise of the gospel. The law reveals to people their sin as rebellion against God and as deserving his wrath and punishment. Although, as pointed out earlier, they can see themselves as sinners—and a sinner of the deepest dye, at that—people will still try to excuse themselves and imagine that they can somehow "make it" in God's sight by reformation, or a new life, or atonement for their actions by some kind of self-sacrifice. The law removes this delusion from them and shows them to be people who are completely lost without God's help and grace.

The gospel brings to faith, allaying the fears of conscience, and comforting the troubled and anxious heart. It is the gospel alone that brings about the end that God desires in the sinner: faith and being reconciled to him. That is why Lutherans often use the terms "Word of God" and "gospel" interchangeably—which is not the case with "Word of God" and "law."

The Spirit's Witness to Christ

In the third chapter, we spent some time on the place of Jesus Christ in the total picture of the Christian's faith. We spoke of his person and said that in an indivisible unity, he is true God with the Father and true man (that is, truly human like us). Where Christ is, there God is, and there the human being is. We spoke of his work of redemption, his sacrifice for the sinful and rebellious human race, by which a new relationship was created between God and the human race. In this great act of God in Christ, the Holy Spirit was not absent. The gospels tell us that Jesus was conceived by the Spirit. It tells us that he was anointed by the Spirit at the beginning of his ministry, when at his baptism the Spirit appeared like a dove and settled on him to the accompaniment of the words of the Father: *"This is my Son, whom I love; with him I am well pleased"* (Matthew 3:17 and Mark 1:11). According to the gospel of Saint Luke, when Jesus began his ministry of preaching in Galilee, he preached at Nazareth, using the opening words of Isaiah 61 as his text, and began with the arresting sentence: *"Today this scripture is fulfilled in your hearing"* (Luke 4:16-21)— but the text from Isaiah begins: *"The Spirit of the Sovereign LORD is on me."*

A particular work of the Holy Spirit began after the ascension of Jesus into heaven. As the Son of God entered history with the incarnation, so the Spirit entered into history at a particular time and in a special way (Pentecost, Acts 2) to carry on the work of Jesus Christ the Son of God. In all this there is noticeable a close harmony between what we call the "persons" of the Godhead.

As the Father sent the Son, and as the Son carried out only what the Father gave him to do (John 5:19,30; 7:17,28; 8:28; 14:10), so the Spirit has no other task and function than to carry on the work of Christ, which he does by accompanying the witness concerning Jesus Christ throughout the New Testament period until Christ comes again. This work of the Holy Spirit is repeatedly spoken of in Saint John's gospel in very clear terms. I shall quote the clearest of them.

> *But I tell you the truth: It is for your good that I am going away. Unless I go away, the Counselor will not*

come to you; but if I go, I will send him to you. . . . I have much more to say to you, more than you can now bear. But when he, the Spirit of truth, comes, he will guide you into all truth. He will not speak on his own; he will speak only what he hears . . . He will bring glory to me by taking from what is mine and making it known to you (John 16:7,12-14; see also John 14:25,26; 15:26,27).

What our Lord says in John's gospel, Paul also teaches in 2 Corinthians 5:18-21.

All this is from God, who reconciled us to himself through Christ and gave us the ministry of reconciliation: that God was reconciling the world to himself in Christ, not counting men's sins against them. And he has committed to us the message of reconciliation. We are therefore Christ's ambassadors, as though God were making his appeal through us. We implore you on Christ's behalf: Be reconciled to God. God made him who had no sin to be sin for us, so that in him we might become the righteousness of God.

In these words we are introduced to the work of Jesus Christ, of which we have already spoken, and to the measures God took to acquaint all human beings with the task Jesus fulfilled. Through this message ("the ministry of reconciliation," the "word of reconciliation") God leads, urges, impels those who hear to believe the message and so to be reconciled to him, so that the work accomplished for them by Jesus might come to its intended goal, their salvation. The gift of salvation can be rejected, and where it is rejected, the work of God has been in vain.

At Work in the Gospel

Now, it is the Spirit of God who is present in the message of reconciliation and in the urgent plea that it be accepted. In the words quoted above, there may even be a direct reference to the Holy Spirit and not merely an indirect one. In the Greek, the italicized words in the phrase: "God were *making his appeal* through us" are a verbal form of the noun Saint John used for the Spirit: "Counselor," literally, "Paraclete." So Saint Paul is there saying the same as Saint John: The work of the Spirit is to carry on in the world the work of the Son by powerfully bearing witness to us as he seeks to work faith in the hearts of those who hear that witness. (See also Romans 10:9-17 for a more complete picture of the whole process, although we do not find there a specific mention of the Holy Spirit.)

It was pointed out earlier that the Word of God is always one, even though it may come to us in various forms, written and oral. The Holy Spirit accompanies this Word in all its forms, as long as it really is the Word of God and not some human perversion of that Word. As the Spirit accompanies the Word, he gives to that Word the divine power that is his, and brings about spiritual life through that Word when and where it pleases him.

A Missionary Faith

What has been said in the last few pages concerning Jesus Christ and his finished work of redemption, of the Spirit as the divine witness to Christ and his work, and of the Word of God as the only vehicle of the Spirit, lays the foundation for the missionary activity of Christianity. Christianity from the start was a missionary religion. The last words in the mouth of Jesus in all the gospels are a missionary command: *"Make disciples of all nations"* (Matthew 28:19); *"Preach the good news to all creation"* (Mark 16:15); *"And you will be my witnesses in Jerusalem, and in all Judea and Samaria, and to the ends of the earth"* (Acts 1:8; see also Luke 24:46-49); and *"As the Father has sent me, I am sending you. . . . Receive the Holy Spirit. If you forgive anyone his sins, they are forgiven; if you do not forgive them, they are not forgiven"* (John 20:21-23).

Christianity is by far the most widely spread religious faith, with twice as many adherents as Islam, which comes in second. Active missionary work down the centuries is the reason for this, although there have been times of widespread missionary indifference. It should not be difficult to demonstrate that proper views and strong convictions on the once for all work of Christ and on the Spirit and the Word must work themselves out in a strong missionary consciousness. *"Salvation is found in no one else* [that is, than in Jesus Christ], *for there is no other name under heaven given to men by which we must be saved"* (Acts 4:12).

The Sacraments: Wondrous Means of Grace

There are other forms of the Word of God that have not yet been mentioned but are of very deep concern to every convinced Lutheran. These forms are known as the sacraments: the sacraments of Holy Baptism and of the Lord's Supper. These forms are unique because in them the Word is associated with actions—sacred acts. In spite of the important features that unite the two sacraments, they will be spoken about separately because they differ so greatly.

In *Holy Baptism,* according to the command of Christ, water is to be applied to those to be baptized, whether infants or adults. Baptism is practiced by all Christian churches. Indeed, where Baptism is not practiced, or is declared to be an unnecessary rite, it is doubtful whether we are in such cases dealing with a Christian church. However, there are a number of more or less grave differences among the churches in how they understand the rite and the execution of Baptism, differences grave enough to cause divisions among them. One of these differences concerns the mode of baptism, that is, whether water may be applied appropriately and in accordance with the will of the Lord in various ways, or whether immersion, complete submersion in water, is a necessary part of the divine command.

Another and more vital difference is whether infants should be baptized as well as adults. This question is part of a wide divergence in the understanding of the gospel. Is Baptism *an act of God,* by which, through the instrumentality of the church as the actual baptizing agent, God bestows the gift of salvation on the recipient? Or is Baptism *an act of human beings* by which they express in a dramatic way the faith which they have in the salvation God has provided in his Son, Jesus Christ? Those who hold the latter opinion reject infant baptism, of course, since only persons of some maturity can give such a decisive expression of their faith.

Baptism Is God at Work

Lutherans belong to those who take the former position. For them, Baptism is God in action, giving a dramatic statement that so-and-so belongs to God—Father, Son, and Holy Spirit—in whose name he or she has been baptized. God, in effect, declares by the act of baptism: "So-and-so is mine. I have redeemed him. She belongs to me."

As such, Baptism is the beginning of the distinctively Christian life. It is possible—and, indeed, it happens often enough—that a person comes to faith before the actual act of baptism, and that such faith produces the desire to be baptized. But Baptism is still the beginning of the Christian life. For it is an objective, out-there act, an act that can be observed, and as such it has a concreteness about it that faith cannot have. Baptism can be observed by everybody; faith, by nobody. What is more, faith is never an unbroken, continuous line, like physical life. Faith may be lost; a person may come to faith again and again. Because of this movement involving faith and because of such repeated acts of faith, no one act of faith can be the beginning of the Christian life.

Baptism as the beginning of the Christian life makes for certainty and assurance. As an act it can be witnessed, remembered by sponsors or other witnesses, recorded on a certificate in black and white. I can be absolutely certain that I have been baptized. But I can never be so absolutely certain that, at such and such a time, I had faith. In contrast with the out-there, objective nature of Baptism, faith is always subjective, something within the soul, within the personality, and so it is something that is subject to doubt and uncertainty. Faith has to be renewed again and again. Lutherans speak of daily contrition and repentance, a daily coming to faith. Faith may be subject to doubt, but **Baptism never fails**. It links believers with the great act of Jesus Christ for their salvation: his death and resurrection. As that event is always valid for the Christian, so Baptism which links the Christian to that event is always valid for the one baptized.

There will be more to say about the matter of faith later. For the moment, it is important to note that there is a confessional aspect to Baptism as well as the aspect I have just spoken about. This confessional aspect is particularly prominent in non-Christian countries. Those heathen who convert to Christianity are known as Christian and are regarded as such only when they are baptized. Baptism is the badge, the mark of being a Christian. Unfortunately, there is very little of this aspect of Baptism in what are reputed to be Christian countries. In these countries, almost everybody is baptized. Almost all have been baptized as infants, yet today very few are practicing Christians. So in very many cases the act of baptism, in effect, turns out to be an empty, almost hypocritical ceremony. However, in that context, when an adult comes to faith and is baptized, confessing the faith of the church openly in front of the congregation, something of the confessional action involved in the baptismal act is recovered and made prominent at that time.

The Lord's Supper

The Sacrament of the **Lord's Supper**, like Baptism, is an institution of the Lord Jesus Christ. The reference to the Supper in 1 Corinthians 11 brings us closer to Jesus historically than any other action or word reported of him. Jesus instituted the Supper just before his death, probably in A.D. 30.

Since Paul writes of the Supper in the middle of the first century A.D., less than 25 years separate this reporting from the actual event. But, as Paul says in 1 Corinthians 11:23, he is passing on a tradition already formed, a fact which closes the gap still further. (Theologians who dispute the institution of the Lord's Supper by the Lord Jesus Christ seem to be banging their heads against a wall.)

Sad to say, the Lord's Supper has been at the center of even more divisions in the Christian church than Baptism. This is a particularly distressing fact because the Supper, according to the Lord's intention, was to be a sign of unity in the church. Saint Paul writes to the Corinthians: *"Because there is one loaf, we, who are many, are one body, for we all partake of the one loaf"* (1 Corinthians 10:17). And in Lutheran Communion services, it is common to hear the pastor say just before the actual communion takes place: "The peace of the Lord be with you always." Blame for division at the Lord's Table is not to be distributed equally and in blanket fashion over all the churches. The greatest blame falls squarely on those who have taken the Lord's words of institution to mean something different from what the Lord intended. It is also true, however, that all churches have in various ways contributed to the division begun initially by false teaching. At times they have not presented the position of other churches fairly and accurately. They have allowed debates on doctrine to be infected with personal animosity. They have also presented to other churches at various times and places an uncertain and ambiguous picture of their own position when professed doctrine has been contradicted by a practice inconsistent with the doctrine.

What the Lord's Supper Is

It is a strange fact that the biggest debate concerning the Supper has been on what the Lord's Supper is. Like Baptism, the Lord's Supper is, first of all, not a doctrine, but an action.

What makes the action of the Lord's Supper different from that of Baptism is that the action is one accompanied by a definition or an explanation. In the Lord's Supper, we do not merely have the action of eating bread and drinking wine (which would correspond exactly to the applying of water to a person being baptized). Rather, the action of eating and drinking in the Lord's Supper is united with a statement of Jesus declaring what is being eaten and drunk. The words of Jesus in themselves are clear enough: *"This is my body"* is the statement attached to the eating of the bread; *"This is my blood of the [new] covenant"* or *"This cup is the new covenant in my blood"* are the words attached to the drinking of the wine.

The Teaching of the Real Presence

Now, it should be plain that nothing of any consequence can be said about the Lord's Supper until we are sure of what we are doing, or what is going on, as Christians eat and drink. Lutherans who are true to their Confessions take the words of Jesus at their face value: "[The Sacrament of the Altar (This is another expression for "the Lord's Supper." "Holy Communion" is also often so used, but for me it is an inferior term)] is the true body and blood of our Lord Jesus Christ, under the bread and wine, for us Christians to eat and to drink" (*Small Catechism*). Or to use the words of Article X of the *Augsburg Confession*: "Concerning the Lord's Supper it is taught that the body and blood of Christ are truly present and are distributed to those who eat at the supper of the Lord. They condemn those who teach otherwise."

In brief, at a confessionally Lutheran altar, the pastor distributes the body and blood of the Lord to those who commune, for the communicants to eat and to drink: "Take, eat; this is the body of our Lord Jesus Christ . . . Take, drink; this is the blood of our Lord Jesus Christ shed for you." And all those who receive what is offered there eat and drink the body and blood of the Lord. "All" includes both believers and unbelievers, confessional Lutherans and other Christians. The Lord's Supper of Catholic churches (that is, the Roman Catholic Church, the Eastern Orthodox, and High Church Anglicans) also is a supper of the body and blood of the Lord.

How it can be that what is plainly bread and wine is at the same time the body and blood of the Lord, Lutherans do not try to explain. They take the words of Jesus as they stand, as he said them, and they dispense with further questions and speculation. This is not the case with such other Christian groups as those just mentioned. The Roman church, for example, has traditionally explained this mystery by the theory of transubstantiation, a theory that has, in turn, led to other views of the Sacrament which Lutherans reject. However, we need to appreciate that the essence of the Sacrament is not destroyed by these speculations.

A completely different view of the Supper is that of the Reformed or Protestant churches. Here the words of Jesus are taken in a figurative sense, so that what is eaten and drunk is bread and wine, and nothing else. However, it *is* insisted that partaking of Jesus' body and blood be done in faith.

Now, this is a very different view from the Lutheran view outlined above, and so what we have in the church on earth as a whole is, in effect, two different meals. To put the matter as plainly as possible, it may be said: At Lutheran and Catholic altars, what is distributed and received with the mouth by all communicants is the body and the blood of the Lord, in keeping with Jesus' own words taken as they stand. What is received at other altars by all communicants is bread and wine, as the official declarations of these churches expressly declare. No amount of clever talk or compromise formulas or astute approximations of *yes* and *no* can bridge the gap between the two understandings of Jesus' words. There is no middle road here even though many have tried to find one.

The Supper's Value and Purpose

I turn from what the Lord's Supper *is* to its value and purpose. For Lutherans, the Lord's Supper is a particularly precious gift. They fight for it, as they do for the gospel or for the truth of justification by faith. They do so because it is the same gospel presented in an especially intimate form. In fact, a very good case can be made for the view that the teaching of Saint Paul concerning the person and work of Christ is really only a drawing out and expansion of the implications of the simple words with which Christ instituted his supper. The Lord's Supper is our Lord's instruction to his disciples and the church concerning his person and work, the source of the apostolic proclamation of the gospel.

First of all, the words of Jesus in the institution of the Lord's Supper, when understood to say that his body and blood are truly present in the bread and wine of this sacrament, teach us to think correctly about the incarnation. The incarnation is that action by which the eternal Son of God became a true man: *"The Word became flesh* [incarnate] *and made his dwelling among us . . . full of grace and truth* (John 1:14). To the end of time, whenever and wherever the Supper is celebrated, Christ is present; his body and blood are distributed, received, eaten, drunk. In other words, Jesus, the Word made flesh, remains the Incarnate One forever, everywhere present and powerful in his flesh as true man. Jesus is God in the flesh, and not only while he lived on earth like other people. **He is so still today and will remain so to all eternity.** It is so easy to think of Jesus as a mere person of the past, as some great figure in history, like Socrates, for example, or the Buddha. But the words of Jesus in the Supper, telling us that he gives us his true body and blood in, with, and under the bread and wine, make it impossible for us to think of him in this way. How can Jesus be a person only of the past when his body and blood are given whenever the Lord's Supper is celebrated?

Secondly, in the words of the Lord's Supper we receive instruction on the meaning of Jesus' life and death for us. Jesus clearly spoke of his body being "given" and his blood being "shed." The word concerning the blood is a plain reference to his death, and the reference includes the thought of a violent death. The preposition "for," especially in Paul's language, expresses the thought of a vicarious death, a death suffered in the place of all people. This manner of speaking of Jesus' person in terms of "body" and "blood" suggests the idea that his death was a sacrifice. In the Bible, we have "flesh and blood," "flesh and bones," "body and soul" brought together often enough, but the combination "body and blood" is a rare one. The separation into body and blood happens especially in the sacrificial act, and so Jesus is very probably hinting in these words that his death was a sacrifice. Jesus points also to the great purpose behind his vicarious sacrifice. His sacrifice is a gift for all human beings: *"given for you";* it is *"for the forgiveness of sins";* it is for the establishing of a *"new covenant"* of reconciliation and peace between God and man. Put all this together, and we have the gospel of the atonement in a nutshell. It is not too much to say that Paul's teaching of the work of Jesus Christ is merely an unfolding of Jesus' words by which he instituted the Lord's Supper.

Thirdly, although the words of institution do not clearly teach the second coming of Jesus, it is a truth that Jesus taught clearly in connection with his supper, as is plain from an examination of Matthew 26:29; Mark 14:25; Luke 22:18; and 1 Corinthians 11:26.

Finally, in the Lord's Supper we can note how both past and future are united in the present. By eating and drinking Christ's body and blood in the Supper, we are linked in time with his sacrifice carried out so many years ago. The Supper spans the gap of over nineteen and a half centuries lying between Calvary and ourselves by giving us *now*, at this time and place, the body given into death and the blood shed *then.* And as for the future, the Supper is an anticipation of the heavenly banquet. (See the passages just referred to.)

The Supper in Christian Piety

Because of its very special nature, the Lord's Supper has generated the highest and most profound expressions of Christian devotion and piety in liturgy, in music, and in elaborate ceremony. But a danger lies in this development, no matter how commendable the reasons behind it might be. There is the danger that the expressions of piety and devotion might come to be regarded as the chief thing in the Sacrament—that the celebration takes precedence over what God is giving and offering to his people.

To speak of the Lord's Supper as being a *sacrifice,* as well as a sacrament, could be cited as an example of this wrong development. This is the case with the Roman Catholic view of this sacrament. For that church, the Mass is first and foremost a sacrifice, an offering to God by the church, that is, by human beings. Lutherans also sometimes like to speak of the Supper as a sacrifice; however, by that phrase they mean that the praises with which the Sacrament is received, and in which it is embedded, are an offering to God. But it is important to notice how ambiguously the word *sacrifice* is used in that case. The regular aim of the word in normal usage is to describe something that people give up, a service that they render at some cost to themselves. Nobody in everyday life thinks of thanks or praise as such a sacrifice; it is only in the sphere of Christian worship that that meaning is to be found. But the rendering to God of thanks and praise is in no sense a giving up of something to God. The praises surrounding the action of the Lord's Supper are nothing but expressions of faith, expressions of our joyful acceptance of the gift offered—just as all Christian worship is always receiving, never giving. In the Lord's Supper also, justification is through faith and through faith alone. The essentials of this sacrament are still there, even if the celebration is as bare and meager as when it was first celebrated by our Lord in Jerusalem so long ago.

Alike but Different

The various means of grace—Word (gospel), Baptism, and Lord's Supper—all have the same content and purpose. They are all signs and assurances of the gracious heart and attitude of God toward sinful mankind. At the same time, it is necessary to note the ways in which these means of grace differ from one another. Only Baptism is the mark and sign of the beginning of the Christian life; it is administered to the individual once and for all time, and it is never repeated. The gospel (Word) and the Lord's Supper are the regular food of the Christian on his path through life to its end and to the coming of the new age. The Word is heard again and again, remembered repeatedly, and read regularly. So also, the Lord's Supper is celebrated throughout the Christian's life. But there is a decisive difference between hearing (or reading) the gospel and celebrating the Lord's Supper. Hearing or reading or remembering the Word can be, and often is, an individual matter. But the Supper is never an individual matter; it is always the church of God, Christ's disciples as a body—his body—which communes and receives this sacrament of the body and blood of the Lord.

The Nature of Faith

Faith has been mentioned repeatedly in the preceding pages of this book, but a description of faith has not yet been given. There has been no description of the nature of Christian faith compared to faith as it is generally understood. This is a short task which must now be attended to.

Sometimes, "faith" can be used in the sense of a creed, as when the pastor says, "Let us confess our faith in the words of the Apostles' Creed." Faith in this sense is something outside of us, something objective, something that can be described, like a table or a map or anything we can point to. This has not been the meaning of the word as it has been used so far in this book. Faith has been used in a subjective way. That is, it has been used to describe a movement or an attitude inside us, something within the human personality, something like such words as *love, fear, hatred,* and so on.

It is this subjective idea of faith which will now be described a little more fully. In general terms, faith is a combination of knowledge and confidence. No trust or confidence is possible in what is not known; on the other hand, it is also possible to have a knowledge of something or someone without trust in it or him or her. As knowledge and trust, Christian faith is parallel to all sorts of faith: faith in democracy, in communism, in a certain political party, in one's homeland, in beauty, in oneself. But Christian faith has special characteristics that put it in a class by itself. It is distinct from all other human experiences of faith.

The human experience of faith, which I will refer to as "faith generally," is a product of human thinking, willing, deciding. If such faith is taken seriously and is not adopted by chance or mere inheritance, then what is said by Simmias, one of the characters in Plato's dialogue *Phaedo*, is a pretty apt description of such faith. Talking about the big questions of life, Simmias makes the following remarks:

> I feel myself, how hard or rather how impossible is the attainment of any certainty about questions such as these in the present life. And yet I should deem him a coward who did not prove what he said about them to the uttermost, or whose heart

failed him before he had examined them on
every side. For he should persevere until he has
achieved one of two things: either he should dis-
cover, or be taught, the truth about them; or, if
this be impossible, I would have him take the
best and most irrefragable of human theories,
and let this be the raft upon which he sails
through life—not without risk, as I admit, if he
cannot find some word of God which will more
surely and safely carry him.[3]

Christian Faith: God's Gift

Christian faith, however, is not like this.
There is nothing examinable or discoverable about
what Christians believe, that is, nothing humanly
examinable or discoverable. The Christian teaching
strikes human reason as quite foreign and alien—
even fantastic. As Saint Paul says, *"'No eye has seen, no
ear has heard, no mind has conceived what God has pre-
pared for those who love him'—but God has revealed it to
us by his Spirit"* (1 Corinthians 2:9). So Christian faith
is a gift from God, wholly so, and not in any way the
product of human intellect, or ingenuity, or any
human powers and abilities. *"No one can say, Jesus is
Lord,' except by the Holy Spirit"* (1 Corinthians 12:3).

When these differences between "faith generally" and Christian faith are clearly kept in mind
and allowance is made for them, we can see that
Christian faith shares the nature of "faith generally."
The reader can satisfy himself on this score by look-

ing at Paul's description of the faith of Abraham in Romans 4, or at the way the writer of the letter to the Hebrews pictures faith in chapter 11 by citing a number of examples of people of faith or, finally, at the letter of Saint James, especially chapter 2. These descriptions are immediately understandable, and they fit in perfectly with the human experience of faith in general.

Some of the more important aspects of faith may be mentioned. Faith is certainty; it is the opposite of doubt. Doubt is an enemy to be overcome, never a friend to be welcomed. Doubts do come to a Christian, but they must be conquered by faith, lest faith be destroyed altogether.

Faith also determines one's action. Faith, we may say, is action, not mere talk. That a person has faith can be demonstrated to others and to self only by the fact that the person lives and acts as though the faith professed is really right and true. A claimed faith, which is not matched by a life in keeping with that faith, is not faith at all; it remains a claim and nothing more. This is the important fact about faith insisted on by Saint James in his New Testament letter, and also by Saint Paul when he speaks about the judgment of God according to works in Romans 2:6.

To make a final point, faith is not in any way the ground of salvation. It is pure reception of the gift of God's grace, of salvation already there in completion. Faith is needed for such reception, for whoever does not believe will be condemned (John 3:18,36). The salvation offered by God is complete, perfect, not to be added to by any human act. Accordingly, faith does not make salvation complete; it receives salvation as a completed gift. And *"whoever believes and is baptized will be saved"* (Mark 16:16).

So, let me summarize this chapter. All that has been maintained in the first five chapters about God and what he has done and about the life which he makes possible for the sinful human race is brought to us by the Word (gospel) and the sacraments. The Holy Spirit, who always accompanies these means of grace with his power, leads those who hear the Word, who are baptized, and who receive the body and blood of the Lord in the bread and wine, to believe and to trust in the truth of what is declared. As long as they do not by unbelief resist the Spirit's guiding, they are led by him to ever deeper and stronger faith. The salvation won by Jesus Christ is offered powerfully by the Word and the Spirit and by faith is made the Christian's own. Such a one becomes and is a saved person.

CHAPTER SEVEN

CONCERNING ME AND OTHER CHRISTIANS

In the opening paragraph of this book, I made the statement that the choice for me was between being a Lutheran and an Epicurean. That sentence could be understood as implying that only Lutherans are Christians. This is not at all the implication I want to make. But further explanation is necessary.

All Christian denominations, as far as I am aware, confess the reality of the "one, holy Christian and apostolic Church" of the Nicene Creed. From now on I shall refer to this as the *Una Sancta.* (These are the Latin words for *one* and *holy* in the Nicene Creed statement.) Lutherans too confess their faith in the Una Sancta, but to them this confession means something far different from what it means to almost all other Christian churches.

The Body of Christ

For almost all churches, the Una Sancta is directly connected with the visible churches—things that everybody sees and knows about. This external church is in disunion—also something that everybody can see and know about. It is generally held by churches that the union of all churches and unity among them is necessary for the church and for the world. The ecumenical movement of this century has been striving for this with very great energy. To state the case very roughly, the Una Sancta, according to the common opinion, would be this visible church in its ideal state. But regardless of how individual churches might like to state it, the Una Sancta is always understood by them as something visible. There are big differences among the churches on this point. The Roman Catholic Church, for instance, simply identifies itself with the Una Sancta: The Una Sancta consists of all those who are in fellowship with the bishop of Rome, the pope. Other churches do not make such a claim; rather, they see themselves as parts or branches of the Una Sancta, pledged to unite the one and holy church as it ought to be.

Lutherans committed to the Lutheran Confessions hold the Una Sancta to be hidden here on earth, hidden within the visible churches, but not identical with them; not identical with any one church nor with any combination of churches. More specifically, Lutheran teaching on the church is closely related to the material of the previous chapter, the material dealing with the means of grace. The Una Sancta is found where these are found, and Lutherans accordingly often refer to the means of grace as "the marks of the church."

The Marks of the Church

Since the Holy Spirit does not work through error or falsehood, it is only the pure teaching of the

Word and the right administration of the sacraments that are marks of the church. So the Lutheran believes and knows the Una Sancta to be present where the marks of the church are present or are to be found. He knows and believes this because of the promise of God that the Spirit through these marks of the church, the means of grace, will bring people to faith in Jesus Christ. Where people are joined to Christ through faith, there the church is. All who believe are Christ's, united with him and the Father and the Holy Spirit. They are members of Christ's body, and that is the New Testament definition for the Una Sancta.

Where the marks of the church are present, even when they are in competition with error and falsehood—as they are in most or all churches—there Christians will be found. So the Lutheran does not deny the name Christian to other church bodies where the essentials of the Christian faith are proclaimed. He expects that the Holy Spirit will bring people to faith also in those churches that must be described as erring churches when judged by the standard of the Word of God.

On the other hand, where the marks of the church are found in their purity, or in something approaching purity, the Lutheran does not expect that all people congregated around such marks of the church will be Christian. Word and sacraments are not automatically effective means for making

Christians, for converting people to Christ. The Spirit still works faith when and where he pleases in those who hear the gospel. Human beings always have the power to resist the power of the Spirit in the means of grace, no matter how truly these means are made use of.

Why Be a Lutheran?

But the Lutheran remains Lutheran because in the Lutheran church that remains true to its Confessions, each one has found a true witness to the marks of the church. Here the gospel is proclaimed in keeping with the Word of God; here Baptism is performed and understood in accordance with the mind of its institutor; here is the real and genuine Sacrament of the Altar. These marks of the church the Lutheran wants, keeps, defends, dies for; these cannot be given up. Union with other Christians can only be on the basis of the true marks of the church.

It is the spirit and genius of Lutheranism to be liberal in everything except where the marks of the church are concerned. Church government, liturgy, history, church traditions, the names and trappings of office, and so on—these have only human value and are, in the long run, indifferent matters, finally unimportant. But over against the gospel and the sacraments, the Lutheran is unyielding. Here the Lutheran stands on holy ground—off with all secular shoes and secular ideals! There can be no playing around with this material, no denial, no compromise, no giving way, no surrender, for by these things each Lutheran lives; they constitute the very breath of life. Take them away, and the Lutheran is done for, gone, destroyed. Every man and every woman will fight for his or her life and fight for it desperately; the true Lutheran man or woman fights for his or her life also—the gospel and the sacraments, that is. Only a person who thinks like this is a true Lutheran at heart.

The Lutheran Church's Mission

The marks of the church determine the mission of the Lutheran church in the world. It is in the world to bear clear, genuine, unambiguous witness to the gospel of Jesus Christ and to the sacraments he instituted: Baptism and the Lord's Supper. It is there to make this witness both to those who are Lutherans and to those who are not, both to Christians and to non-Christians, for it is entrusted with the very Word of God, the Word of salvation. The Lutheran church is there to nurture its members—and all others who will listen—with these divine means of grace; to lead its members—and all others who will listen—into the kind of life described in earlier chapters, especially chapters 2, 4, and 5; to bring them to a stronger faith, a more perfect love, a more joyful hope. It sees its role in the world to be that expressed in the words of the writer of Psalm 32: *"I will instruct you and teach you in the way you should go; I will counsel you and watch over you"* (Psalm 32:8).

At this point in the argument, discerning readers will probably think that I have been guilty of a grave omission in my account of the mission of the church. They will be aware that most churches in the world and especially the large representative bodies like the World Council of Churches and the Lutheran World Federation—as well as the pope of Rome—have assumed for themselves a leading role in the endeavor to bring about a better world. The various churches make solemn declarations on a whole host of important concerns: on war and peace, on poverty and health, on justice and human rights, on freedom and the role of women in society. The churches have much to say on the proper action of governments in all quarters of the globe, calling upon them to change such-and-such a policy and enact such-and-such reforms. Knowing all this, it may well be a matter for wonder that the present description of the mission of the church has failed to speak of such activity as part of that mission.

The answer is that the confessional Lutheran just does not consider these matters to be part of the mission of the church. A distinctive teaching of Lutheranism comes up here: the doctrine of the two kingdoms (although this traditional view has also been discarded by a great part of the modern

Lutheran church). It is clear that we need to look at the rationale of this teaching more closely.

The Church's Commission

The church has been charged with only one commission by its risen and ascended Lord: to preach the gospel of the forgiveness of sins, life, and salvation. All four gospel accounts conclude with a scene in which the risen Lord appears and gives his disciples directions as to what they are to do at his final departure from them. These directions are couched in quite different words, but the meaning is demonstrably the same. Take these words in Saint John's gospel as one example:

> *Jesus said, "Peace be with you! As the Father has sent me, I am sending you." And with that he breathed on them and said, "Receive the Holy Spirit. If you forgive anyone his sins, they are forgiven; if you do not forgive them, they are not forgiven* (John 20:21-23).

In Matthew's gospel the commission is stated like this:

> *All authority in heaven and on earth has been given to me. Therefore go and make disciples of all nations, baptizing them in the name of the Father and of the Son and of the Holy Spirit, and teaching them to obey everything I have commanded you. And surely I am with you always, to the very end of the age* (Matthew 28:18-20).

The apostle Paul puts the situation in yet another way:

All this is from God, who reconciled us to himself through Christ and gave us the ministry of reconciliation: that God was reconciling the world to himself in Christ, not counting men's sins against them. And he has committed to us the message of reconciliation (2 Corinthians 5:18,19).

There is something absolutely right and proper and even inevitable about this whole state of affairs. If the world has indeed and in fact been reconciled to God by one mighty, historical event, what else remains but that this fact be made known to all those affected by it? We might say that there simply can't be any other task for the church of believers than the one given to it by the Lord of the church.

The words of the Lord recorded in Saint Matthew point to another task of the church inherent in that of proclamation, a task that affects the behavior of those who have heeded the gospel call to be reconciled to God and have become Christ's disciples. All such disciples are to be guided to live a life of love as long as they are in this world. The will of God for them as contained in the Ten Commandments (the law of love spelled out in specific terms), in the example of Jesus, in the instruction for Christian living contained in Jesus' words (see, for example, the Sermon on the Mount), and in the admonitions to be found in the New Testament letters constitutes this guide. When the church uses this guide to guide and direct its members, it teaches its members to observe all that Christ has commanded.

The Teaching of the Two Kingdoms

The proper ordering of the world has been committed by God to various structures of society that he himself has ordained. The chief of these are the home and the state. The home is the natural unit of society, where children, to a great extent, can be trained for life by the man and the woman who brought them into existence. The "powers that be," the governments of the various independent countries, no matter how they might be organized and no matter how good or bad they may be, are also ordained by God; they are his way, his necessary way, to preserve humanity. Without the law and order and, to a large degree, the protection afforded by a government or a state, the human race would soon destroy itself in one big suicidal holocaust. All human beings are included in these structures of society, Christians included.

However, the functions of the church and of the structures of society differ in their natures and in how they are carried out. The church's function is carried out by the proclamation of the Word and the administration of the sacraments, the Spirit being the power at work in them to bring about the desired result of faith and the new life. For the ordering of society, the necessary factors are reason or common sense and the judicious exercise of force and compulsion. It will be seen at once that we have here a special case of the difference between law and gospel, which was referred to in the previous chapter.

Now, law and gospel cannot be brought together into one teaching. They are "more than contradictory" (Luther). Confusion of law and gospel in the form of an interlocking of the functions of church and state can only lead to evil and harm to society. The most common evil is that either state or church becomes an oppressive power.

There is a strong ingredient of sheer rationality and obvious common sense about the teaching of the two kingdoms, so strong, in fact, that I am amazed that so many non-Lutherans show such evident annoyance when they write about it, or that so many Lutherans seem so ready to apologize that it is part of the Lutheran heritage. Why shouldn't the church simply say: "The preaching in all the world of the gospel of salvation and what flows from it is our task, which fully takes up our resources; the work demanded in bringing about a better world is something for other human organizations to attend to. We have this very special work to do, and we are going to concentrate on it for it is good and necessary for itself. The other work is necessary too, but that is not the purpose of our organization."

Of Christians—Not of the Church

There are hundreds of clubs and societies in the world devoted to certain aspects of human life, organizations that bring together different groups of people in order to make possible a furthering of their particular interests. Must all of these too make the bringing into being of a better world an essential part of their program? The suggestion is preposterous. Everybody knows that involvement in one or more of these clubs devoted to special interests does not prevent its members from working for world betterment at the same time. There is no contradiction between the specific organization and its special aim, on the one hand, and the necessary aim of world betterment on the other. Why, all of a sudden, the indignation when Lutherans say that the church has been given a special commission by the Lord that does not include action for world betterment, and that the state is a different institution of God with a purpose that does include such action. For the Christian, involvement in one organization does not preclude involvement in another; Christians are involved in both. Christians are members of the church and citizens of the state and can act in both areas of life and in both capacities.

We can pursue reason and common sense in this matter in another direction: The church and church leaders have no special competence in matters of government and the measures needed to bring about a better world. What is needed here is a knowledge of human beings, of personal and social ethics, of economics and politics, and all the rest—not forgetting a knowledge of what is possible as well as of what is ideal and desirable. In all parts of society there are people—religious and non-religious—who possess competence in these areas. The church, as church, has nothing to give to the solution of the problem of world betterment that is any more to the point than what any intelligent Jew, Hindu, Muslim, or atheist who has the facts and knows his business can give. The proper ordering of society belongs to the law, and in this matter we don't even need our Bibles and the ethics of Jesus. Heathen folk and unbelievers also show the work of the law written in their hearts.

The Church's Unique Task

If what we have said just now is true, we face a further consequence. Those who forsake the task of proclaiming the gospel of the forgiveness of sins in order to devote themselves to a different message are in the process rendering themselves quite useless and irrelevant as church leaders. The more any church moves in that direction, the less reason for existence it has.

And, conversely, the church that sees its only mission to be proclaiming the gospel is saying something the world will hear nowhere else; it is not merely repeating in its own way what can be heard in every conceivable quarter. And, so Lutherans are convinced, it is proclaiming a message that human beings neglect at their peril but which, if accepted, serves their true good here and their eternal salvation hereafter.

As the Lutheran church that is true to its Confession carries out its task, it sees itself not as some new phenomenon in the world, arising at the time of the Reformation, but to be in continuity with the apostolic church in its original doctrinal purity. And it carries out its task in view of the last judgment, knowing that however weak and sinful it is in itself and in its members, the gospel it has preached will be acknowledged as the truth by the all powerful Judge himself.

To God—Father, Son, and Holy Spirit—be all glory now and in all ages to come! Amen.

STUDY NOTES

Introduction and Chapter 1 "What Is to Become of Me?" (pp. 9–24)

1. Page 9. How does Hamann defend his conviction that "the only logical alternative to his commitment to the Christian Lutheran faith [is] Epicureanism in its popular form: 'Let us eat and drink and be merry, for tomorrow we are dead'"?

2. Page 11. According to Hamann, what does the sentence "I am a Lutheran because I am a Christian" assert?

3. Page 17. What questions do all religions attempt to answer?

4. Page 21. How does Hamann see the universal belief in some form of life after death as a basic truth for the defense of the faith?

5. Page 22. Why does Hamann say that the "question concerning God's existence is **not** the radical question"? See Psalm 14:1.

6. Page 24. What is the "vital question" according to Hamann? See Psalm 130:3,4.

Chapter 2 "How God Thinks of Me" (pp. 25–34)

1. Page 25. Hamann notes three words—favor, consideration, affection—that are descriptive of God's grace. Read the following Bible passages, noting how each passage accents Hamann's definition of grace:

Psalm 67:1,2
Isaiah 30:18
Micah 7:18-20
John 1:16,17
Ephesians 1:5-8

2. Page 26. God's attitude toward us in his Son, Christ Jesus, is not wrath or indifference but grace. In other words, "it is the Christian conviction that God is *for us*–in every way." According to Romans 8:31-39, how do we know this?

3. Page 26. What images come to your mind as helpful in understanding the biblical word *justification?* See Romans 3:21-26.

4. Page 28. As a result of God's justification (that is, his regarding us as righteous for the sake of his Son), we are given a new "status, position, and relationship" with God. Hamann notes, "The Christian is described as being *a child of God* and, as such a child, also *an heir.*" We are not children of God by nature, but "objects of wrath" (Ephesians 2:3). God has adopted us in Christ through Baptism. How do the following passages make this point?

John 1:12,13
Galatians 3:26-29
1 Peter 1:3-5

5. Page 28. Hamann notes that "forgiveness of sins" and "reconciliation" are two important synonyms for justification. How are these words used in the following passages:

Psalm 32:1,2 (also Romans 4:4-8)
Romans 5:9,10
2 Corinthians 5:18-21

6. Page 29. What does Hamann mean by the "dark side of the whole matter" of our justification?

7. Page 29. How would you answer the accusation that the Confession of Sins in The Common Service is "too negative"?

8. Page 30. Contrast the biblical view of man in Romans 3:10-12 with that of Sophocles.

9. Page 32. While many non-Christians are willing to assert the general corruption and evil of humanity, it is only from the Scriptures that we know the true depth of our sin. How does Hamann describe "the truly terrible nature of sin"?

10. Page 32. How is the miracle of justification offensive to human reason? See Romans 5:6 and Luke 19:10.

Chapter 3 "God for Me in Jesus Christ" (pp. 35–53)

1. Pages 36,37. Following the lead of C. S. Lewis who argued that the only three options as to the person of Jesus Christ are "liar, lunatic, or Lord," Hamann argues that Jesus' words reveal that he is God. Skeptics sometimes argue that in the gospels Jesus never claims to be God. How would you answer this assertion?

2. Pages 38–47. According to Hamann what are the three main ways in which the life of Jesus has been assessed?

3. Pages 42,43. What happens when "Christ as example" is separated from the fact that Christ is the Savior?

4. Pages 45–47. Hamann notes that the New Testament uses three major words in its picture of Jesus: *redemption, sacrifice,* and *reconciliation.* Taken together what do these three words tell us about our Lord's work?

5. Page 48. How does the New Testament describe the life of Jesus? See Philippians 2:8 and Hebrews 5:7-9. What are the "two sides" of Jesus' obedience?

6. Page 49. Read 1 Corinthians 15:1-5,17. What is the importance of Jesus' resurrection? Also see Romans 4:24,25.

7. Page 51. What are the "three realities" that are dealt with in the biblical doctrine of redemption?

Chapter 4 "Through Christ I Am a Free Person" (pp. 54–68)

1. Pages 54,55. Read Romans 8:31,32. According to Hamann, what is the "Christian logic of these verses"?

2. Page 55. How does Job demonstrate the "stance of faith" in Job 1:21 and 2:10?

3. Page 56. In what sense does the First Article of the Creed build upon the Second Article?

4. Pages 56,57. What is the theme of Luther's *The Freedom of the Christian*? What are the implications of this freedom for day-to-day Christian living?
5. Pages 57,58. How does faith free us from worry and care? See Matthew 6:25-34. Also note Galatians 2:20 and Psalms 4 and 16.
6. Page 59. How are the "worth and dignity" which we have in Christ different from humanistic concepts of "self-esteem"?
7. Pages 60–62. What shape does our freedom take in relation to the neighbor?
8. Pages 62–64. In what way does our freedom in Christ impact the way we go about our daily work? Also see Ephesians 4:28 and 6:5-9.
9. Pages 64–66. How does the gospel free us to enjoy the gifts of God's creation? See 1 Timothy 4:1-5; Romans 14:14-23.
10. Pages 66–68. What does Hamann mean by describing freedom as "flowing from faith"?

Chapter 5 "How I Face Death and What Lies Beyond" (pp. 69–81)

1. Page 69. What does Hamann mean by the statement, "There is something incomplete about the gift of God as it affects me here and now"?
2. Page 69. Hamann notes that "The experiences of believer and unbeliever in this life are precisely the same." How does Ecclesiastes 2:13-16 bear out this fact?

3. Pages 70–72. God's kingdom is both "now" and "not yet." See Luke 17:20 for a statement of the "now" of God's kingdom and Romans 8:23 for a statement of the "not yet" of God's kingdom. What does Scripture teach us in this paradox?
4. Pages 72,73. What can we say about heaven? See 1 John 3:2.
5. Page 74. What will our Lord's final judgment do?
6. Pages 77–80. How are we to understand the New Testament passages regarding the nearness of our Savior's return? (See 1 Peter 4:7 for example.) Note 2 Peter 3:3-13.
7. Page 80. Read 2 Thessalonians 3:6-12. What wrong conclusion did some early Christians draw regarding the return of our Lord?

Chapter 6 (Part I) "God's Word and My Faith" (pp. 82–92)

1. Review the Explanation to the Third Article in the *Small Catechism*. How does Romans 10:6-17 describe the creation of faith?
2. Page 83. What is the connection between the Holy Spirit and God's Word? See Psalm 33:6 and John 14:23-27.
3. Page 84. Read Hebrews 1:1,2. How does this passage teach us to understand revelation?
4. Page 84. What are the various forms of the Word of God?
5. Pages 86,87. In what sense are the law and gospel completely contradictory in nature?

6. Page 87. Notice the significance of the Holy Spirit's witness to Jesus Christ in each of these episodes in the gospels:
Luke 1:34,35
Matthew 3:17
Luke 4:17-21
John 16:7-14
7. Page 89. How is the Spirit's work described in 2 Corinthians 5:18-21?
8. Page 91. What does Hamann mean when he says that Christianity is a missionary religion? See Matthew 28:16-20 and Luke 24:46-49.

Chapter 6 (Part II) "God's Word and My Faith" (pp. 92–109)

1. Read Matthew 28:16-20. What is Baptism according to this passage?
2. Page 93. Within Christendom, there are basically two differing views of Baptism. One view sees Baptism as an act of human beings. The other group sees Baptism as God's work. How do the following passages describe Baptism?
Romans 6:1-10
Acts 2:38,39
1 Peter 3:21
Titus 3:4-7
Ephesians 5:26
John 3:1-8
Colossians 2:12

3. Page 95. According to 1 Corinthians 11:23-26, what is the Lord's Supper?
4. Pages 100–103. How does Hamann describe the value and purpose of the Lord's Supper?
5. Pages 105–107. What is the nature of faith?
6. Page 107. How do each the following passages describe an essential aspect of faith?
   1 Corinthians 12:3
   Romans 4:13-25
   Hebrews 11:1-3
   James 2:18

Chapter 7 "Concerning Me and Other Christians" (pp. 110–122)

1. Pages 110,111. What do Lutherans mean by their confession of the *Una Sancta?* How does this differ from the Roman Catholic Church's usage of this term? How does the Lutheran confession of the church differ from the way most Protestant churches think of the *Una Sancta?* Note the comment of Hermann Sasse: "The presence of the church is not dependent upon our faith and profession, but upon the real presence of Jesus Christ" (*Here We Stand,* p. 182).

2. Pages 111,112. What are the "marks of the church"? The *Augsburg Confession* states of the church: "This is the assembly of all believers among whom the Gospel is preached in its purity and the holy sacraments are administered

according to the Gospel. For it is sufficient for the true unity of the church that the Gospel be preached in conformity with a pure understanding of it and that the sacraments be administered in accordance with the divine Word" (*Augsburg Confession*, Article VII:1, Tappert, p. 32). How do the marks of the church make the unity of the church manifest?
3. Pages 114,115. What is the mission of the church according to confessional Lutheranism? See John 20:21-23; Matthew 28:18-20; 2 Corinthians 5:18,19.
4. Pages 119–122. How is the proper distinction between the law and the gospel at the heart of the teaching of the two kingdoms? See Article XVI of the *Augsburg Confession*.

These study notes were written by Rev. John T. Pless.

ENDNOTES

[1]These two quatrains are numbers 68 and 69 of the 1895 edition of Edward Fitzgerald's version of *The Rubaiyat of Omar Khayyam*. Later on, I shall quote also numbers 73, 57, and 58 of the same poem. The poem of Fitzgerald is in every way an English poem, based on selections and combinations of the original Persian stanzas.

[2]Translation by Benjamin Jowett found in *The Portable Plato*, (New York: The Viking Press, 1948), p. 329. The Greek reference is Book II, section 361 b,c.

[3]*The Portable Plato*, p. 233. The Greek reference is Book II, section 85 c,d.